Elephants
and
Quaker Guns

Elephants
and
Quaker Guns

NORTHERN VIRGINIA:
CROSSROADS OF HISTORY

Revised Edition

Jane Chapman Whitt

VANDAMERE
PRESS

Published by
Vandamere Press
A division of AB Associates
P.O. Box 5243
Arlington, VA 22205

Revised Edition
Copyright © 1984 by Vandamere Press

Second Printing
September 1994

ISBN: 0-918339-03-0

Library of Congress Catalog Number
85-051890

First Edition Published 1966
by Vantage Press, Inc.

Design and Composition
Big E Typographics, Reston, VA

Manufactured in the United States of America

FOREWORD

It was as a newcomer twenty years ago that I first heard some of the history of the communities around Bailey's Crossroads and Munson Hill. Fascinating folklore included tales of Indians, circuses, and Civil War skirmishes.

My start on *Elephants and Quaker Guns* began in 1963 when I was asked to do the Bailey's Elementary School Yearbook and to include in it a short history of Bailey's Crossroads. After I confirmed through research at the National Archives, Library of Congress, and other sources that folklore was indeed based on fact, the journals of former local citizens, biographies, letters, official records and anecdotes began to combine into a narrative.

I obtained copies of maps, ranging from the earliest one known of Fairfax County, about 1748, to the 1965 edition of "Street Map of Washington," published by the Prince Lithograph Company, Inc., Arlington, Va. I am pleased to be able to share these maps with you.

Especially helpful during my research were the publications of the Somers, New York. Historical Society, the Arlington Historical Society, the Fairfax County Historical Society, and the Columbia Historical Society, Washington, D.C. I especially appreciate the assistance given by Miss Pat Carey, Curator of the Virginiana Room of History, Fairfax Public Library; Colonel J.B. Mitchell, Curator of Fort Ward, Alexandria, Va.; and Mr. Elmer Parker of the National Archives, who helped in locating sources of information.

I also deeply appreciate the assistance of the following persons without whose help the stories in *Elephants and Quaker Guns* could not have been compiled:

Mr. and Mrs. Munson Lane who shared family stories and manuscripts in their possession, including a letter written by President Lincoln.

Mrs. Jonathan T. Rorer, President of the Historical Society of Somers, New York, who provided much information about the man for whom Bailey's Crossroads was named, Hachaliah Bailey.

Miss Marguerite Gordon Bailey and relatives, Mrs. Marie Bailey Cartwright and Mr. George Gordon Bailey, who shared memories of family background.

Mrs. Dora Bailey Terrett who remembers her grandmother, Mariah Bailey, and uncle, George F. Bailey.

Mr. W. Parkhill McGowan who provided the letters written in 1865 by a Federal soldier stationed at "Camp Bailey's X Rds."

Mr. Leonard V. Farley, Curator of the Hertzberg Circus Collection in the San Antonio, Texas, Public Library, who did a great deal of research for me on America's early circus man, George F. Bailey, whose circus P.T. Barnum acquired and called The Greatest Show on Earth.

I also appreciate the kind help given by Mrs. Milton Shepperd, Mrs. Lily Mortimer Bailey, Mrs. Irvin Payne, Sr., Mrs. Mary Gordon Hobart, Mrs. H.W. Wolford, Mrs. Arthur Parsons, Mrs. Margaret Stetson, and many, many others.

I appreciate the assistance and encouragement given by Colonel Quintin Lander, Mr. and Mrs. Donald Wilkins, Mr. Leonard Furbee, and Mr. John Gott who read *Elephants and Quaker Guns* in early manuscript form and offered helpful comment.

Very special thanks go to my husband, Colonel Samuel S. Whitt, who edited the manuscript. Without his help and encouragement the task of writing could not have been accomplished.

Special thanks go also to two young artists: Joyce Peeks, who drew from life the Church Hill House before it was destroyed for a new building in 1964; and James Montgomery, who drew Maury, the hundred-room house, from photographs and descriptions. Thanks also go to photographer Richard M. Sparks II.

Through *Elephants and Quaker Guns* we have tried to give some of our heritage its well-deserved niche in history.

Bailey's Crossroads, Virginia   JANE CHAPMAN WHITT
November 1, 1965

FOREWORD TO THE SECOND EDITION

This revised edition of *Elephants and Quaker Guns* updates the book by providing background on the phenomenal growth and development of Northern Virginia in the last two decades. It also gives information on the location of historic places blurred by contemporary development and left unmarked by local authorities. The main body of the book is essentially unchanged as it is the history of the area.

JANE CHAPMAN WHITT

September 20, 1985

CONTENTS

CHAPTER ONE

Introduction

Northern Virginia today is as much a part of the District of Columbia as it is a part of the State of Virginia. While legally and geographically part of Virginia, the area's economy and population are inexorably linked to the nation's capital. It is indeed hard to imagine the rural Northern Virginia of the 18th and 19th centuries, to envision a time when Washington D.C. did not exist and when Alexandria was the only significant population center in the area.

With the founding of Washington, D.C., the focus of Northern Virginia shifted gradually away from Alexandria toward the District. Throughout the 19th century, Northern Virginia was engaged primarily in agriculture. Its communities were mostly occupied with providing farm and dairy products to markets in the city of Washington. Its tallest buildings were the steeples of its churches. In the late 1800s and early 1900s, there were increased visits by residents of Washington to enjoy that which Northern Virginia still retained, the ambience best described as "clean county living." During this time, some of the larger old plantation homes were converted into boarding houses and became known to Washingtonians as desirable "summer getaway" places. One of the best known was named *Maury* at Bailey's Crossroads described in that era as "the house with a hundred rooms."

With the advent of the automobile in the early part of the 20th century, Washingtonians began to acquire homes in Virginia, perhaps the most popular suburb being Arlington's Glen Carlyn where a resident named Moses Ball had built a mill on Four Mile Run in the 18th century. The southeast boundary of his land was adjacent to property referred to in the 1790s by the owner George Washington as "my upper tract" to differentiate it from his downriver estate, *Mount Vernon.* Washington's designation is apt today because this area is now known as Skyline Towers, one of the highest of Northern Virginia's residential and business complexes.

With the end of World War II, major suburban development began to flourish. For Federal employees and military families thinking of some easy trail to the Pentagon or Washington, Northern Virginia provided the answer. At first this meant the purchase or rental of an old farm house, but soon there were apartments and developments. In quick succession subdivisions like Glen Forest, Sunset Manor, Ravenwood, Munson Hill (which had its crest scalped by bulldozers), Lake Barcroft, and Aura Heights were built. Dozens more were sandwiched in and around these. Military installations and businesses devoted to research and development were established through out the area. The pastoral scene vanished tree by tree and the hodgepodge of modern suburban life emerged.

Very quickly, the rural nature changed during the 1950s and 1960s. Sections of Arlington and Alexandria which had a head start began to boom. By the mid 1970s, the term "close-in suburbs" had come to be defined as anywhere inside or near the Capital Beltway. Seemingly without end, the suburbs have continued their sprawl past Manassas, Woodbridge, Dumphries, and even as far as Leesburg.

The story of Northern Virginia is often lost in the history of the nation. In a less fast-paced area, landmarks and historical sites would have been saved and refurbished. In Northern Virginia, they have too often been bulldozed and paved over. This book is a local history of the area, and where national figures have played major local roles, they have been included. Their often more famous national exploits have been left for others to describe. It is a story of citizens, who in other cities not overshadowed by the proximity of the nation's capital, would be remembered as more than the name of a subdivision or a hill.

Above all, this is a story that requires the reader to view familiar sites through the mist of history. It requires that the reader see places such as Seven Corners as a Civil War fort, Tyson's Corner as a simple tavern at a crossroads, Ballston as the site of a military balloon ascension, and Bailey's Crossroads as a summer retreat far from the heat for Washington. The map on the following page has been prepared to help the reader find locations discussed in this book. It provides the reader with Northern Virginia's major roads as they appear today along with approximate locations of past historic sites.

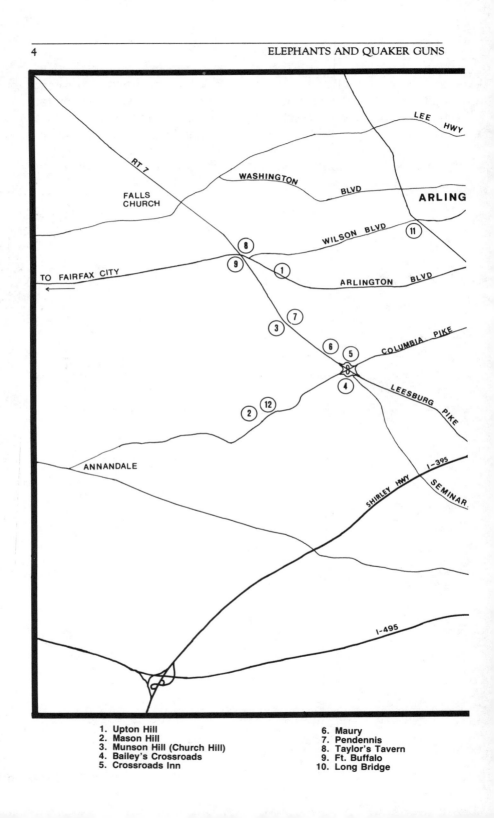

1. Upton Hill
2. Mason Hill
3. Munson Hill (Church Hill)
4. Bailey's Crossroads
5. Crossroads Inn
6. Maury
7. Pendennis
8. Taylor's Tavern
9. Ft. Buffalo
10. Long Bridge

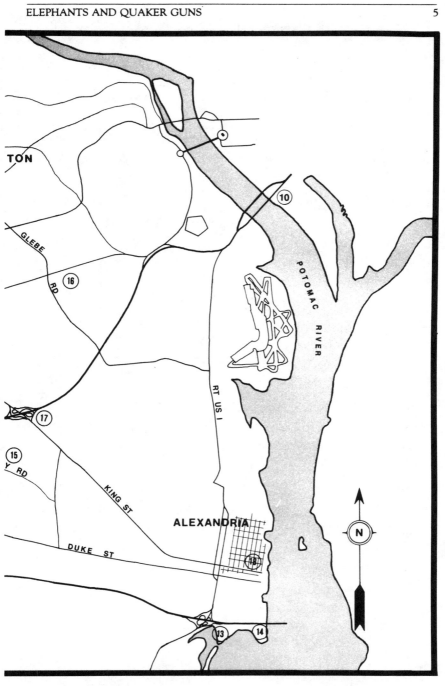

11. Balls Crossroads
12. Barcroft Mill
13. Great Hunting Creek
14. Jones Point
15. Episcopal Seminary

16. Ft. Richardson
17. Ft. Ward
18. Carlyle House

CHAPTER TWO

Indians and Settlers

When the first European settlers arrived in the Northern Virginia area in the early 17th century, they found that the area was already inhabited by the Necostin tribe of the Piscataway Indians. The Indians had fishing towns at Arlington and Great Hunting Creek, and agricultural tracts and quartzite tool manufacturing sites near springs in the Falls Church area. They traded fish for the furs of Indians to the north.

Woodsmen and sea merchants who worked for King Charles II's commercial interests were soon carrying on a brisk fur trade with the Indians to the north who were great hunters of buffalo and beaver. Records tell of northern Indians with birchbark canoes filled with furs meeting English traders at Hunting Creek. Because of Potomac Falls, *portage* of fur-laden canoes was necessary. Carrying canoes overland could have been accomplished via pathways from the falls to the headlands, then via footpath or waterway to the river.

Potomac Path, a land route used by Indians, traders, colonists, and later by postal couriers, extended from Jamestown to Great Hunting Creek where it branched into several paths, one extending to today's Rosslyn and another, called Great Eastern Ridge Road, continuing up a higher ridge — probably old Seminary roadbed — to the headlands and then northwestward to a mountain gap (Leesburg Pike).

The site of Washington, D.C., had been used for generations by numerous Indian tribes as their meeting place for councils. This annual gathering was festive with games, feats of skill, and pageantry. Ceremonial dances in full feather and shell regalia took place near modern Rosslyn. The Indians used footpaths which linked today's Rosslyn, Arlington, and Alexandria with the high plateau between Falls Church and Bailey's Crossroads. Tribes of Powhatan's Confederation apparently held part of this plateau. A strong local tradition is that Powhatan Springs near Seven Corners once belonged to that famous chieftain.

There was inevitable rivalry between Indians and whites for control of the land, especially land as strategically situated commercially and militarily as were the headlands. The local Indians, who had been acquainted with Europeans since 16th-century visits by Jesuits, were generally friendly to settlers; but they and the colonists were both wary of the Indians to the north.

The earliest settlers, Cornish-speaking men from southern England and Scotland, planned to garrison and stock a "ffort on the Potomack" with other militia to be garrisoned *"at other places fronting upon the enemy at or near John Mathews."*[1]

The remains of a fort, built before 1670, are still to be seen in the basement of the 1752 Carlyle House in Alexandria. An outpost for this fort may have been at Munson Hill which was a high point overlooking the Powhatan Springs area and the council lands at Washington and Rosslyn. This may account for the earliest name associated with the hill, Pendennis, a Cornish word which meant "headland of the fort."

The Governor of Virginia tried to maintain friendly relations with the northern Indians because of the King's lucrative fur trade, but there was conflict and bitterness between them and the settlers. Once, after marauding Indians had murdered some Upper Potomac settlers, a party of armed white men hurried in pursuit and shot several friendly Necostins by mistake.

In 1675, the murder by Indians of Robert Hen, overseer of a Mathews plantation, so incensed the settlers against the Governor and his policies that it precipitated the events called Bacon's Rebellion. Later, Colonel John Washington led the colonial militia against Indians to the north. By the late 1670s, all Indians, including Necostins, had been removed to lands elsewhere. Except for occasional harassing raids, white settlements no longer were menaced by Indians.

It is occasionally heard that Seven Corners had been an Indian trading post in colonial days. No document pertaining to a post at this exact site can be located. However, its location at a bend on a high place on old Great Eastern Ridge Road makes it a likely spot for such use even in the earliest years.

Seven Corners has a history as a stopping or meeting place. In the early 1800s an inn, called an Ordinary, belonging to the Adams-Minor family, existed there, and for many years Taylor's Tavern operated at the same site. In 1906 John D. Payne, mayor of Falls Church, lived at the site which was then known as Payne's Corners.

Following the Indian exodus after the period of Bacon's Rebellion, a declaration was issued by the Colonial Government:[2]

An Act Lycensing Trading with the Indians

"Inasmuch as total prohibition of trading with Indians is hurtful to His Majesty's Colony and inhabitants thereof ... Indians shall have free and full liberty to come amongst us and bring in commodities. Such marts or fairs shall continue for fforty days and noe longer ... the place for the marte or ffaire in Potomack to be appointed and sett down by the justices of the peace in Stafford [Fairfax] County — the 30th day of April and the 30th day of September.

"... Indians meeting at any of these marts or faires shall not carry or travel with armes, except for carrying home such arms or ammunition as he should purchase at said marts.

"Clarks of each mart and faire may take to himself 1/20 part of all Indian Commodities there Sould, trucked or traded or dealt fur. ... Noe person or persons shall be hindered from entertaining Indians in their house."

It is ironic that Indian fairs were held in the area. Tribute may have been paid unconsciously to the Indians both in the Civil War name of Fort Buffalo, perhaps given in honor of the first Federal unit to fortify it, and in the use of the area today as a modern shopping center.

People, Plantations, Ports and Progress

Land grants mentioned in records pertaining to the mid-17th century involve the Mathews, Brent, and Howsing families. Howsing sold his 6,000-acre tract which bordered the Potomac from Rosslyn south to Great Hunting Creek to John Alexander. The Brent family of Maryland and Northern Virginia, who were related to local Indians through a family member's marriage to a Piscataway Indian Princess, owned a small tract at Great Hunting Creek extending inland. The John Mathews tract, which was to be granted in 1685 to Fitzhugh as 22,000 acres named Ravensworth, also lay in the area and extended to a corner boundary near the heights known today as Seven Corners.

The headlands in Bailey's Crossroads-Seven Corners area provided a landmark for many of the patents. Flowing from these headlands were the main water sources, Great Hunting Creek and Four Mile Run. These tracts and others became known in 1664 as Upper Potomac of Stafford County. Some of the area was under cultivation for tobacco.

The meager records of the 18th century describe plantations from Great Hunting Creek to Falls Church. By 1742 there were enough residents to create Fairfax County. The first seat of county government was on Great Eastern Ridge Road near Tyson's Corner.

Descendants of John Alexander owned much of the land drained by Four Mile Run and used its estuary where it flowed into the Potomac River for loading ships with tobacco and wheat crops. The wealthy and powerful families of Fitzhugh, Lee, and Carter controlled their own export interests at other Potomac estuaries. An association of Scottish merchants controlled an enterprise south of Great Hunting Creek. There were many marriages made in the European baronial manner between sons and daughters of local gentry to create complex family empires.

Early landholders in the Bailey's Crossroads area were Thomas Pearson and his son-in-law, Gabriel Adams, co-owners of a patent obtained in 1707 from Thomas, fifth Lord Fairfax, and his wife, Lady Culpeper, whose ancestors had obtained royal title to the lands of Northern Virginia. Pearson and Adams were prominent men with many business interests. In 1729, Thomas' son, Simon Pearson, patented a 330-acre land tract which extended approximately from Bailey's Crossroads to the Carlyn Springs area. When Simon died in 1733, his daughter Susannah, who became Mrs. John Alexander III, inherited this tract which was known as Alexander's property for many years.

A descendant of Gabriel named William Adams built a wood-sided brick house for his family at Munson Hill about 1750.

Members of the Adams family were early active members of the Falls Church Episcopal congregation. William built and operated a grist mill on Holmes Run where three tributaries of Great Hunting Creek joined at deep cuts in the land. The crumbling walls of this mill may still be seen near Barcroft Dam.

William Henry Terrett, who married Simon Pearson's daughter, Margaret, owned 1,000 acres of land which extended across Holmes Run and Seminary Road. The Terretts owned numerous slaves and a great deal of plantation equipment as did the Adams family. Terrett's plantation was *Oakwood,* built near Bailey's Crossroads and, according to Terrett's will, they also owned a house on property next to the river in 1755. Lots which they bought when Alexandria was founded in 1749 were at Fairfax and Duke Streets. By 1750, everyday life had become typically tidewater Virginian with a network of country roads connecting plantations to the port at newly chartered Alexandria City.

There was much excitement when General Braddock's British troops arrived, along with colonials, at the military staging area Cameron near Great Hunting Creek for battle with French and Indians to the northwest. Construction was begun on new roads for military use and a headquarters was provided for Braddock by Alexandrian John Carlyle, who in 1752 had built a magnificent home over the walls of the old waterfront fort.

Men wrote wills preparatory to going west with Braddock and Lieutenant Colonel George Washington, but there was no real concern over danger to the area's plantations. By the late spring of 1755, two units of Braddock's Army struggled across the Great Eastern Ridge Road to the mountain gap. Their campaign was not successful and the northwest area was not gained until the Revolutionary War.

The New Nation

The contributions of many famous Northern Virginians during the period of the revolution, the Articles of the Confederation, and the writing of the Constitution are already well documented. With the adoption of a new constitution and the selection of George Washington as the first President, in 1789, the new nation began to emerge. On a local level, the transition from colony to state went remarkably smoothly. Land ownership which had evolved from the original royal patents and grants remained unchanged.

Land surveying, and hence ownership bounderies, in the earlier periods of Northern Virginia's history were far from an exact science. Existing records go back over 325 years. The records are maintained in several locations depending on county boundaries of the period. Fairfax County was established in 1742 from land taken from Prince William and Stafford Counties. A section of Fairfax County, today known as Arlington County, including portions of modern Alexandria, was given to the U.S. Government in 1801 as part of the District of Columbia. In 1847 the Federal Government returned the land south of the Potomac River to Virginia as Alexandria County. The city of Alexandria separated from the county in 1870, but not until 1920 was Alexandria County renamed Arlington. Appendix A traces a typical patent through 120 years of its history.

After George Washington had served two terms as President of the United States, he retired to his Fairfax County home, *Mount Vernon.* He worked hard to improve his riverside estate and increase his land holdings, adding several tracts to the west of Alexandria. The accumulation of tracts, which he referred to as "my upper tract" (later to be called Custis' Washington Forest), extended from Four Mile Run to the vicinity of today's Skyline Towers.

Washington ran several joint surveys of this land tract with men whose property lines touched his. Surveying the lands of western Virginia for Lord Fairfax had been Washington's first occupation when he was only sixteen years old. During his later years he considered surveying an opportunity for an outing with Fairfax County associates. In his diary, Washington noted two expeditions to survey the Upper Tract[3]:

> "Apr 3, 1799. . . . Went up to Four Mile Run to Run round my land there. Got on the Grd about 10 o'clock, and in Company with Captn Terrett and Mr. Luke commenced the survey on 4 Mile Run, and ran agreeably to the Notes taken. In the evening went to Alexa. and lodged myself at Mr. Fitzhugh's."

> "Apr 4th Recommenced to survey at the upper end where we left off, in company with Colo. Little, Captn. Terrett and Mr. Wm. Adams. . . ."

The ancient tree trunk on display in Glen Carlyn Library, Arlington County, was the white oak on Four Mile Run noted in Washington's survey of Upper Tract in 1799.

George Washington's earlier Alexandrian associates included such men as wealthy John Carlyle who, in addition to having built Carlyle House over the ruins of the 17th century fort, also established a thriving plantation at Fairlington and subleased other farmlands. Carlyle also purchased land near Munson Hill. These outlaying farms and forests produced wheat and lumber. Shipbuilding and milling became the most profitable enterprises. Flour was shipped to the world's marketplaces from Alexandria and its rival port, Georgetown. After the Revolution, the Far East became a major destination for ships from these ports.

A legislative deadlock in 1790 over selection of a Federal capital site resulted in a decision to leave the final selection to the nation's beloved past President. Washington chose the present site of the District of Columbia. He may have recalled stories heard in his boyhood of tribal councils meeting at the site.

Placement of forty boundary markers for the District of Columbia was begun, the first Virginia stone being placed on April 15, 1791, at Jones' Point, Alexandria, during a Masonic ceremony conducted by Washington and other notables. The second stone to be placed (designated Stone #6 marked "5 miles 304 poles") was one-half mile from Bailey's Crossroads at a point exactly southwest from the site of the White House.[4]

Church Hill

The descendants of Gabriel Adams leased or sold much of their land but retained the homestead. During the late 1700s and early 1800s, America was swept up in a wave of evangelistic fervor. The Adams house, owned then by William and his wife, Ann Lawyer Adams, was the place where the Washington area's Methodist Church had its beginnings. Most of Adam's numerous descendants and their spouses, including names such as Watters, Payne, and Lipscomb, were associated with the burgeoning religious impulse of this era.[5] Bishop Francis Asbury visited the family many times and Adams' property on its knoll was called Church Hill. Asbury would conduct services in the parlor to the right of the front door whenever he visited. With new religious convictions, the family at Church Hill freed slaves and employed those who cared to stay as free men.

Elizabeth, an Adams relative, married William Payne of Fairfax Court House village. His route during courtship days would have been the narrow road which connected that area with Church Hill. After Columbia Pike was constructed, these local roads became known as back roads.

The Lipscombs lived in the Church Hill homestead for many years. After relatives named Payne acquired the house, it became known by their name. At some time in the 19th century, the house acquired the desgination, Widow Payne's Dower House.[6]

After William Adams died, his mill on a tract of 25 acres was sold as separate property. In 1849 this property, *Millbrook,* was purchased by Dr. John Woolverington Barcroft from New Jersey. Dr. Barcroft also purchased Arlington Mill from the Custis estate on Columbia Pike at Four Mile Run. He operated these mills for many years, manufacturing flour for shipment around the country. Barcroft built a home for his family on the hill above his Holmes Run mill.

During this same decade, Daniel Gordon from Georgetown, D.C., purchased land now called Culmore. His neighbors, other than Adams' descendants, were the Terretts at *Oakwood* and the Whitings, descendants of John Carlyle who were owners of property near Munson Hill. Gordon's gently rolling farmlands at the foot of Munson Hill were depleted from past use, but he had not come with the intention to farm, but to raise cattle.

Gordon built a large cold storage room over a spring, lining it with wooden planks and covering it with earth. He used it to store dairy products awaiting shipment to Washington. Nearby Spring Branch, fed by his spring and others near Munson Hill, was one of the tributaries entering Holmes Run near Barcroft's mill. Daniel Gordon built a substantial house on a rise in the ground behind today's Culmore Shopping Center. By his first marriage he had two sons, Charles and George Dent Gordon. After his first wife died, Daniel married Amanda Burroughs in 1853, and they had ten children.

CHAPTER THREE

The Baileys and the Munsons

While early Northern Virginia was being settled, one of the regions most colorful families, the Baileys, was still in New York state. In the latter part of the 18th century, Hachaliah Bailey lived in Westchester County, New York, but his business frequently took him to New England where he became well-acquainted with the merchant seamen of Salem, Massachusetts. The maritime business was the first to recover after the country's fight for independence, and the industry leaders were important people. Hachaliah knew Jacob Crowninshield whose fleet led the way to the East Indies, and his brother was a sea captain.

It was merchant seamen such as these who discovered the Chinese desire for ginseng, a medicinal root. To the Chinese Ginseng was what Ponce de Leon had hoped to discover in the fountain of youth, and the Chinese were willing to pay its weight in gold.

When settlers in western Virginia discovered ginseng growing wild in mountain coves, smart merchants were ecstatic and began the trade which brought great wealth to many members of American business life. This was especially true for the Salem sea-merchants who plied the lengthy ocean voyage and those traders whose wagons, filled with ginseng roots, plied the trails between the western mountains and eastern seaports.

In 1796 after a year on the ocean via Cape Horn, Captain Crowninshield returned from China in his vessel, *America*, with a prize cargo that caused as much wonderment among Americans as ginseng did among the Orientals. It was an elephant with her native attendant.

In those days Hachaliah, was a young drover with headquarters at the Bull's Head Tavern in the Bowery, New York City. He wanted the elephant the minute he laid eyes on her and promptly bought her for $10,000. None of the records prove he bought and sold ginseng, but not many Americans in the 1790s except ginseng dealers had that much money. At any rate, he named her Old Bet. As America's first elephant, she was a real curiosity and immediately paid her own way.

Hachaliah's business took him over 300 miles into New England to buy herds of lean cattle which he would drive back to pens near Bowery Tavern to fatten for selling. He took Bet on these trips and on trips into Virginia, exhibiting his big pet at 10¢ a head. Later he acquired horses, bears, monkeys, and dogs which he and his entourage trained to do acts. They traveled by night because the scent of the wild animals, especially the elephant, would frighten horses pulling other carriages. An advance man with a bell would ride ahead on horseback to warn night riders and, incidentally, to advertise that the circus was coming!

Hachaliah called his traveling menagerie an Educational Show. He hired Van Amburgh, the great animal trainer and rider, and for a while he was associated with the financier Daniel Drew (later partner of Commodore Vanderbilt). Bailey made other investments in cattle and steamboats.

Hachaliah's elephant, Old Bet, was touted as having a hide too thick for a bullet to penetrate. Along the trail one day a young farm boy thought he would test this statement and, taking a rifle, aimed and found the assertion false. Old Bet died.

Hachaliah grieved over the loss of Old Bet. He had a statue carved of her with trunk raised, which was gilded and placed on top of a granite shaft before a beautiful new inn he was building in 1823 in Somers, New York. The inn, designed in the Salem manner with pitched roof and widow's walk, was on a turnpike well-traveled by such notables as Washington Irving, Aaron Burr, and Horace Greeley. Hachaliah named the establishment in Bet's memory, *The Elephant Hotel.*

Horace Bailey, a relative, assumed management of the inn which became renowned. The hotel's Register is today considered a veritable *Who's Who* of the early 1800s.

The Elephant Hotel and Old Bet's statue still stand. The building has been declared one of the finest examples of early 19th-century American architecture by architect Edgar Williams, a fellow of the Architectural Institute of America. It has had the good fortune of having been bought and maintained by the township of Somers as its seat of government and a museum.

In the 1820s, Hachaliah became a customer of Phineas T. Barnum, who ran a fruit and confectioner's shop with a sideline of cheap rings, jewelry, and toys, items which Hachaliah probably obtained for circus gimmicks. The continuing relationship between Barnum Bailey was to become one of America's most famous partnerships.

A few years later, financial disaster overtook young Barnum, and he was hired by Hachaliah to run his circus front office at 37 Bowery. This was Barnum's first real taste of circus life. Barnum stated in his autobiography that Hack Bailey was the man he admired the most next to his grandfather.

About this time several New Yorkers joined with Bailey in the exhibition of unusual animals. Also in the 1820s, several men combined shows under the name, June, Titus and Angevine Show, and hired youthful Phineas T. Barnum as their agent.

Later, in 1835, these men and others—a total of 130 showmen, museum owners, and business men—met in *The Elephant Hotel* and incorporated their interest in the Association of the Zoological Institute. Stock value was set at $329,325.00, a very considerable amount in those days. The Institute acquired the Bowery Amphitheatre, which became a famous showplace of old New York, and continued to maintain Bailey's office at 37 Bowery with Barnum heading it.

The Zoological Institute's showmen included such talent as acrobats, clowns, equestrians, and animal trainers. Numerous shows traveled all over the country to give performances. These earliest showmen toured Latin America and traveled regularly to California in the 1830s, long before the Gold Rush began. The best known early winter quarters for circuses were at Danbury, Connecticut.

Hachaliah Bailey's closest business associate was a relative, George Brown who had first helped in the exhibition of Old Bet. Another relative, Benjamin Brown, was one of the showmen who toured the world, frequently facing hazards to obtain unusual animals for the menageries.

The Washington Connection

Washington, D.C., was a regular stopover for these traveling shows. The earliest circus showplace in Washington was Brown's Amphitheatre at 4½ Street near the Capitol which had an adjacent circus lot. A popular performance presented at Brown's and Bowery Amphitheatres in the 1830s was the Grand Equestrian Drama, which featured many trained horses and bareback riders.

Realizing the need for a country place for animal training and wintering quarters in the Washington area, Hachaliah Bailey bought land in Fairfax County, Virginia, on December 19, 1837. The purchase also included acreage lying in Federal territory.[1] The land tract of over 500 acres surrounded the crossing of two important highways, Leesburg Turnpike, which extended from Alexandria to a northwest mountain gap, and Columbia Turnpike, which had been constructed by the Federal Government about 1809. Little River Turnpike, three miles distant from the Crossroads, was a main highway to the west. Hachaliah correctly considered his Virginia purchase to be situated on the pathway to all points north, south, and west. He immediately put his property to circus use.

In 1843, Hachaliah deeded this property not to his son Lewis, but to Lewis' energetic wife, Mariah Snook Bailey.[2] Mariah, who sometimes spelled her name Maria, was known for her business acumen. She and Lewis had grown up in Somers. They had both been circus children and had learned at an early age how to sit and stand while riding bareback, the way of the circus performer.

Lewis and Mariah Bailey and their growing family arrived in the early 1840s to develop the Bailey's Virginia estate. As described in the deed, the boundary of their tract began "near a school house at Whiting's property" and was surveyed in a generally north-by-east, south-by-west direction, touching at the property of Custis and Carlin; then to the edge of a "branch"; then to "Mercer's beginning"; then southwest to Lawrence Lacy's on the south side of old Leesburg Road; then in a roundabout way to the beginning point. The Crossroads lay in the District of Columbia. In 1847, the Federal

Government returned Virginia territory to the state, and it became known for a while as Alexandria County. Bailey's deed to the property called it "that certain parcell of land patented by Simon Pearson in 1729."

The "branch" referred to in the deed is the upper Long Branch which flows from Seven Corners past Munson Hill through Glen Forest, culminating at Four Mile Run near Glen Carlyn. Previous owners had constructed a dam on Long Branch to create a lake large enough for small boats and a stock of fish. When the lake froze in the winter, ice was cut and stored in the well aperture and springhouse for use all summer.

Lewis and Mariah found there was already a handsome old structure behind the Crossroads in the area now called Glen Forest. The house, having every aspect of a mansion, was called *Maury or Moray.*

Maury was colonial in design with a center hallway typical of early Virginia homes. Bricks of *Maury's* central portion were hand-made as were the bolts and hinges. The three-story dwelling had a hand-dug basement. A well had been hand-dug 35 feet deep and lined with handmade brick.

The family had brought furniture by wagon caravan from New York to furnish their home . At an auction in Alexandria they acquired Duncan-Phyfe tables which had been in Mount Vernon. (These later were restored to Washington-Custis estates by a daughter-in-law, Mrs. Horace Upton Bailey.)

A long, rambling, frame travern-type inn at the Crossroads was improved, and barns and carriage houses were built nearby for vehicles. The inn's patrons were travelers, circus personnel, and drovers en route with cattle to Washington markets.

Mariah loved flowers and began a circular brick formal garden which was a showplace by Civil War days. Crepe myrtle, althea, roses, forsythia, lilacs, boxwood, honeysuckle, and wisteria grew against a background of oak, holly, spruce, and walnut trees. The Baileys did not own slaves, but they did sometimes hire or rent slaves from Mr. Dulin of nearby Falls Church, Virginia.

Lewis continued the traditional family business of cattle-raising and obtained the milk concession for Washington's leading hotel, the Willard. He did not consider himself a farmer, however, raising only what was needed for the inn and the circus clientele.

Everyone looked forward to the arrival of the circus. Several of the Zoological Institute's circuses were famous for their Arabian

horses and skillful riders, many from abroad. They had rediscov-
ered, as had English circuses, the idea of the ancient Greek-
Roman Hippodrome, a circular riding exhibition using trick
horse-and-rider acts, gaily-decorated chariots, and costumed
charioteers.

One of the shows with which the Baileys were closely associated was the Aaron Turner Circus which began the use of large
canvas tents to shelter the Hippodrome and spectators. George F.
Bailey, Hachaliah's nephew, who was born in New York in 1818,
married the daughter of Aaron Turner. He took over management
of the Aaron Turner Circus which toured throughout the south and
visited Cuba and South America. During these years, P.T. Barnum
frequently traveled with the Turner Circus.

Other members of the Institute traveled with shows along local
turnpikes and may have visited at the Crossroads during the early
19th century. This number included Van Amburgh and John
Robinson, featured Hippodrome performers who could ride four
horses at once, Dan Rice, the clown, Jake Posey, who managed
the forty-mule teams needed to pull show wagons, and circus
agent Frederick Bailey, Lewis Bailey's brother.

One of these circuses acquired ten Senegalese pachyderms in
the 1850s. At that time they comprised the world's largest group of
trained elephants. Elephants were the biggest drawing card,
attracting attention wherever they traveled.

Many work horses were needed in addition to show horses. One
team of horses had the unique task pulling a hippopotamus tank
over muddy trails from town to town. Fourteen horses were needed
to pull this one wagon. The local blacksmiths were busy men
during the winter months, preparing horses for tour. Many skilled
blacksmiths settled at the Crossroads to ply their trade.

In addition to horses, elephants, and an occasional hippo, there
were dromedaries, zebras, monkeys, dogs, lions, tigers and
giraffes (the Baileys and Browns brought the first giraffes to America in the 1840s). Animals were housed in barns outfitted with
restraining pens for wilder beasts behind the Crossroads Inn.
Fields of grain were planted and rabbit snares maintained to provide food for the animals.

A circular riding ring near the Bailey barns was the site for
Hippodrome training. Whenever a circus was at Bailey's, the air
resounded with noises new to the countryside. There were the
commands of the trainers, many with foreign accents, and cracks

of the whip to emphasize directions. Fiddlers were hired to provide music. After the mid-1850s, calliope music accustomed animals to cues. It was a circus all for free in the barns, at the riding ring, all day long, paradise for one sister and nine little Bailey boys.

Mariah and her children loved these days and observed acts during training. Sometimes they rode the elephants. They knew the horses by name. The fun really came after circus caravans had pulled out for tour, for then there was time to bring out their own horses and teach them a few tricks.

Although Hachaliah spent some time at the Crossroads during the earliest years of Bailey ownership, his declining months were spent at *The Elephant Hotel* in Somers, N.Y., talking to the many vistors who congregated there daily. Hachaliah Bailey, America's enterprising pioneer circus showman, died in 1845.

Timothy Munson Buys Pendennis

Another family who was to have considerable local prominence, especially during the Civil War, was the Munson family. In 1851, Timothy Bishop Munson, a Presbyterian from Leicester County, New York, with his wife Nancy Meacham, and children, Timothy B. Jr., Ira, Annie, Daniel, Miles, and Lucy, bought the tableland of Munson Hill. The farm was 260 acres extending from Holmes Run to Wilson Boulevard, including land formerly belonging to the Carlyle-Whiting family. Munson's new home was called *Pendennis.* It stood in a grove of trees on Leesburg Pike opposite the entrance to modern Nevius Street.

Mrs. Munson died the year after they bought the Munson Hill farm. Timothy, who came from a family talented in plant culture, continued to develop a fruit tree nursery. Together with his sons, Miles and Daniel, he successfully planted and developed a grove of peach trees, a fruit not native to Virginia but known to have been imported and grown sucessfully on the plantations of Pearson and Adams in the 18th century. As they prospered, the Munsons acquired several fine horses. His sons once went to New York and purchased two beautiful horses which they rode back together, an adventure the brothers cherished in later years.

The following paragraphs are excerpts from the biography of Timothy Munson[3]:

"Timothy Munson was plain and unpretending in dress and speech, but he was a man of more than ordinary intelligence.

While he was gentle and conciliatory in his disposition, he had strong convictions and was firm as a rock when principles were involved. Though moderatley educated he was fond of reading, ambitious to ascertain truth, and possessed of wisdom. He was a man of unquestioned integrity and sterling worth, and though not formally a professor of religion, he always led his family to the sanctuary."

About the Munson Hill farm, Myron Munson wrote:

"Munson's Hill is conical in shape, elevated about 100 feet above the surrounding country, and situated about 5 miles in direct line from Washington. From the summit, which contains about one acre of table land, there is a good view of the capitol, Washington monument and several miles of the Potomac River, and in the west, on a clear day, the Blue Ridge can be seen distinctly...."

"...Proper buildings were erected, grain, hay and vegetables were raised, while the nursery business and sheep raising were also pursued by the father and sons. With industry and frugality the family prospered."

In 1859, Timothy started the building of a new Georgian style frame house across Leesburg Pike from *Pendennis* to accommodate his family. At that time, politics and news from old friends and relatives back in New York were uppermost in his mind. He took an active part in the election campaign of 1860, taking a stand unpopular with most neighbors. He led an armed party of men to vote for Lincoln on November 6, 1860, and thereafter felt it was necessary to leave his home in Virginia for awhile. He spent the winter months of 1860-61 in Washington with relatives who lived in Georgetown.

Myron Munson wrote the following about Timothy's political life:

"...He was careful to avoid giving offense to the proslavery neighbors by whom he was almost entirely surrounded. When slaves came to him with grievances against their masters he would kindly advise them to return and endure patiently. Yet he was firm in expressing his convictions as to the right of all men to freedom. In politics he was an ardent Republican and took active interest in the election of Lincoln. In November he led a party of 7 man, all armed to the teeth, who voted for Lincoln at the risk of their lives. Immediatley after he was obliged to leave the State of Virginia and he spent the winter of 1860-61 in Washington."

Voting in the United States before the Civil War was not uniformly done by secret ballot. In some polling places, the *viva voce* method prevailed, and groups of local men were known to line up ready to cheer or jeer as a vote was cast orally and repeated by the registrar in a very loud voice. When political issues were hotly contested, those in the minority sometimes had to have ready fists as well as firm convictions.

During 1860, the Washington area was seething with intrigue. Passionate indignation on both sides continued to mount. General Winfield Scott, the aging Commander in Chief of the Army of the United States, upon being forewarned by a citizen of a supposed Southern plan to destroy Lincoln Presidential ballots before they could be counted, roared:

"...Any man who attempted by force ... to obstruct or interfere with the lawful count of the electoral vote ... would be lashed to the muzzle of a twelve-pounder and fired out of a window of the Capitol. I would manure the hills of Arlington with the fragments of his body.... While I command the Army there will be no revolution in Washington!"[4]

CHAPTER FOUR

Secession

It was obvious to many Northern Virginians that if Civil War came, their Crossroads position would make them key participants in the nation's saddest experience. The coming war was an emotional issue for Unionists and Southerners alike. It was a problem that would not go away.

In April 1861, Southern forces fired on Fort Sumter in South Carolina, and several states seceded from the Union. On May 6th, Jefferson Davis announced the existence of war between the seceded states and the North.

Unionists of Virginia resisted secession. The State Government decided a poll should be taken of citizens on Thursday, May 23, 1861, to decide upon the ratification or rejection of "an ordinance to repeal the ratification of the Constitution of the United States of America by the State of Virginia."

The local precincts had a good turnout to vote "yea" for secession. Timothy Munson and many Unionist neighbors, realizing the hopelessness of the case, did not try to vote in this poll of citizens.

The listing of the citizens' vote on the Ordinance of Secession, May 23, 1861, Fairfax County, has been preserved. This record of votes cast has been published by the county and is believed to be the only such listing of a vote concerning state secession still in existence. The only local citizen named Bailey who voted was

William Bailey, a son of Lewis. In 1861 he would have been 20 years old.

After Jefferson Davis' declaration of the existence of war between the seceded states and the North, plans to protect Washington were formulated hurriedly by Federal authorities. There was disappointment but little surprise when Virginia's citizens voted to secede.

Following Virginia's decision to secede from the Union, on a bright moonlit night at two in the morning of May 24, 1861, Cavalry, Infantry, and Engineers crossed Long Bridge (at today's 14th Street) and began the work of fortifying the hills along Washington's southern perimeter. By June 1st, the Federal Army had occupied Alexandria City, Ball's Crossroads, and Columbia Pike to an outpost at Bailey's Crossroads. Federal units were also patrolling Leesburg Pike from Bailey's Crossroads to Falls Church. To quote Carl Sandburg:

"Southern advocates termed the invasion and pollution of the sacred soil of Virginia a northern aggression more infamous than the southern attack on Fort Sumter."

As a measure of the respect in which he was held in Washington, Timothy Munson was sent for twice by President Lincoln and General Scott for consultation. He returned to his home at Munson Hill when the Union Army occupied that locality but was soon obliged to flee after the Bull Run disaster. After the war began, he was often at Washington in council with leading Virginia Unionists. Military operations in Northern Virginia were one reason why Munson was summoned to consult with Lincoln and Scott. It was urgently necessary to know as much as possible about the enemy's local roads and terrain.

The project uppermost in Lincoln's mind became that of restoring the Union. Neither he nor Congress had yet enunciated any statement about slavery in 1861.

Northern sentiment against slavery had been intensified by the writings of Harriet Beecher Stowe and the famous mulatto, Frederick Douglass, and by the stand and subsequent death of John Brown at Harper's Ferry, Virginia. Many Washingtonians in 1861 owned slaves. During the early weeks of the war, many of these slaves crossed the Potomac to be with the new army which was being hastily assembled in Alexandria and parts of Fairfax.

The army had enough problems with the feeding and training of thousands of raw recruits and was in no way prepared for the slaves, men, women, and children, who became hangers-on in the new Federal Virginia camps. There were many cases of hardship among these slaves which became known very soon to the commanders of the Federal troops. The Army of Northern Virginia under General McDowell therefore asked Washington for a directive.

The Federal Army at Norfolk was having the some problem, but these slaves were coming from southern plantations. Rather than permit them to return to the South where it was presumed they would be used to build military fortifications, the Army declared these southern runaways, "war contraband," and decided they would stay with Federal units near Norfolk.

Lincoln conferred about the problem with his Army Chief, General Scott. Scott, it is reported, warned those he talked to that "the name of the President should not at this time be brought before the public in connection with this delicate subject.[2]"

The Battle of Bull Run

During the summer of 1861, the Armies of the North and South gathered strength in Northern Virginia. General Beauregard, Commander of Confederate forces at Manassas, thirty miles from Bailey's Crossroads and General Scott in Wahington issued military orders confining citizens of the North and South to their separate territories. The homeowners between Mannassas and Washington soon discovered they were living in a no-man's land.

Commanders of both armies pored over hastily procured topographic maps and noted the advantages for both offensive and defensive operations offered by the high ground at Upton's Hill, Taylor's Tavern (Seven Corners), and Munson's Hill with their clear views of Washington, situated five miles to the northeast.

Bailey's Crossroads, well-situated on its high plateau beyond the narrows traversed by Columbia Turnpike, was soon a Federal bivouac area and outpost. Military preparations turned the local blacksmith shops into busier places than ever, with cavalry and other military horses brought in for shoeing. Wheelwrights busily prepared army vehicles.

The military occupation throughout Northern Virginia fanned the already hot flames of animosity. Federal leaders reasoned hopefully that occupation of Munson Hill would be far simpler politically because it was owned by a Unionist. But militarily, it was not to be as easy to march into as Bailey's had been.

During the war's early weeks, the crisscrossing of enemy troops at Munson Hill, where a back road from Fairfax entered Leesburg Pike, caused numerous engagements of a minor nature. Munson Hill become an outpost and was occupied first by a small group from one side and then by detachments from the other. Upon seeing the enemy's approach, troops retreated, usually without gunfire to stronger rear positions. For the Confederates, these were toward Annandale and Fairfax and for the Union toward Ball's Crossroads and Alexandria.

As the Union Army increased in size, the North began to believe optimistically that a march to Richmond would bring quick victory. In late July of 1861, Federal troops with cavalry, cannon, and wagons streamed down the roads to the southwest. Civilians, including officials from Washington, drove in their carriages to observe the advance.

The results of the inevitable clash, now called the First Battle of Bull Run, which occurred near Manassas were described in the *Daily Picayune:*

> "... The Northern enemy straggled into Washington dreadfully mangled. My informants stayed at Falls Church the night after the battle. They saw the rear guard come in about 11 at night in horrible condition, hungry, weary and perfectly dismayed ... Our Army is still encamped on the heights overlooking Alexandria and is now really a splendid one and sufficient for anything it may be called upon to do even to the assault of the works on Arlington Heights at the edge of the River.[3]"

For several weeks after this battle, Washingtonians fully expected their city to be invaded. Everyone clamored for news of the war front, but immediately a General Order was issued by the U.S. War Department warning against giving information to the enemy. Newspaper editors clamped down on printing stories from the front lines. Rumors spread about the size of the big Southern Army poised for attack on "the other side of the hills!" Ambitious plans were formulated expeditiously by Lincoln and Scott, aided by young General George McClellan, to erect a 34-mile fortified perimeter with earthworks and batteries around Washington in order to secure the headlands.

In August of 1861, the Federal General Richardson moved up Leesburg Pike from Bailey's with a considerable force of regulars in order to secure the headlands. He knew that Confederate pickets were ranged along high ground between Munson Hill and Mason Hill which were connected by a back road.

Richardson was not surprised by the spate of gunfire which occurred before the Confederates withdrew from Munson Hill. He set his men to work digging entrenchments at two points overlooking Falls Church and Annandale. He was very much aware that the heights overlooking Alexandria where Confederates were poised were less than two. miles distant beyond the trees at Mason Hill.

Family Fortunes

Among the local families in Northern Virginia caught up directly in the movement of troops and intermittent battles, there were many misfortunes and tragic cases of family members pitted against one another in divided allegiance to Union and Confederate causes. The Gordon family was one of those so poignantly divided. Their house at Columbia Pike and Munson Hill also stood quite often in the midst of opposing forces.

Daniel Gordon was traveling during the early weeks of the war to take care of business interests in New York. Quite unexpectedly, he was arrested and interned for some period of time. His family of two older sons by a first marriage and younger children by his second wife, Amanda, living at the Gordon house, were left to manage on their own. Daniel's two older sons, Charlie and George Dent, who had grown up riding on horseback to attend Episcopal High School at Seminary Hill together, were in violent disagreement. George was very much for secession but just as hotly, Charlie was pro-Union. Both boys soon joined the conflict on opposite sides.

Amanda Gordon and her other children were alone as the war quickened and skirmishing began. Several time bullets flew across the Gordon house. In midsummer of 1861, in the midst of a skirmish, a Gordon son not yet in his teens discovered that bullets had penetrated the crib headboard of his six-month-old baby sister's bed. Quickly, he picked up the baby and hurried his mother and younger brothers and sisters to the carriage. He hitched up and drove toward Ball's Crossroads and then back to a friend's farm home near the Arlington-Falls Church border.

At one point during the war's early weeks, George and Charlie visited their home for a few hours. Their leaves coincided. Amanda was caught between the hurt anger of the two young men and was hard pressed to keep the two apart. She had to devise ruses to

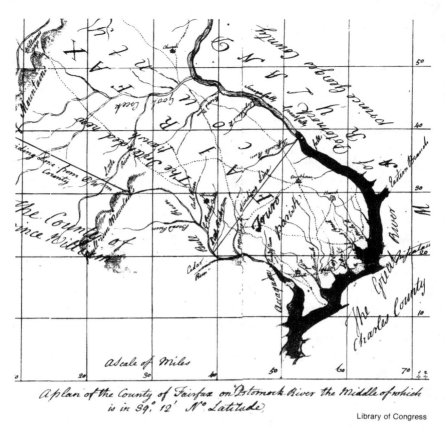

Map of Fairfax County, circa 1748

Church Hill House, 1750-1964

Washington's Upper Tract Survey, 1799
George Washington Atlas, 1932

Old Bet's Statue and Elephant Hotel, Somers, N.Y.

19th Century Bareback Riders of the Circus Hippodrome

Quaker Gun at Munson Hill. Artist, A. R. Waud, 1861

Munson Hill with fort erected by Garibaldi Regiment.
Harper's Weekly, Nov. 23, 1861

Sutler's Cart at Bailey's Crossroads. Artist, A. R. Waud, 1861

Troops on Munson Hill looking toward Fort Buffalo.

Photographic Saloon, Balls Crossroads, VA
Harper's Weekly, Nov. 23, 1861

Lowe's Balloon "Union" at Munson Hill. Harper's 1861

Difficulties of Teaming. Artist, A. R. Waud, 1861

J. E. B. Stuart and Cavalrymen. Artist, Frank Vizetelly, circa 1861
from *Civil War Times Illustrated Magazine*, Gettysburg, Pa.

Fairfax Episcopal Seminary, Alexandria, Va. Photographer Matthew
Brady in foreground, 1861.

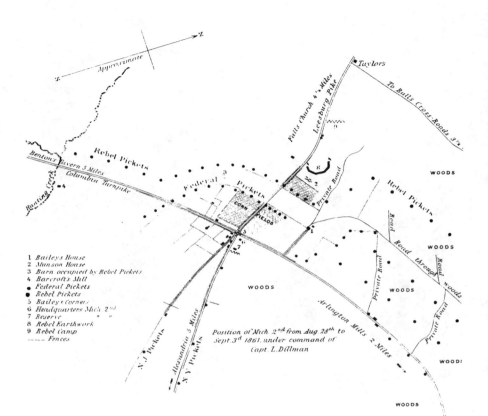

SKIRMISHES NEAR
BAILEY'S CROSS-ROADS, VA.
August 28-30.
1861.

Map of Union and Confederate Positions, Bailey's Crossroads area
August 28-30, 1861

The Great Review at Bailey's Crossroads, Virginia, on November 20, 1861, sketched for Harper's Magazine "by our Special Artist from the Top of a Barn."

39

The Secretary of the Treasury,

Washington.

Lincoln's Letter—the Envelope

Executive Mansion
Dec. 13. 1861

Hon. Sec. of Treasury

My dear Sir:

I am very anxious that some employment shall be found for the young lady, bearer of this — Please see her & her brother, who are driven out from Munson's Hill —

Yours truly

A. Lincoln

Lincoln's Letter
Courtesy of Mr. and Mrs. Munson Lane, Arlington, Va.

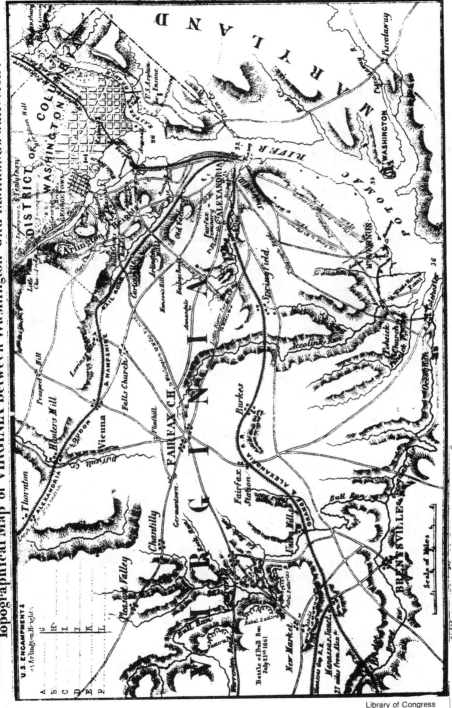

Topographic Map of Virginia between Washington and Manassas,
circa 1862

Grand Army Review, 20th Army Corps., Sherman's troops arriving, looking down Pennsylvania Avenue towards the Capitol.

Capitol Hill looking toward Northern Virginia

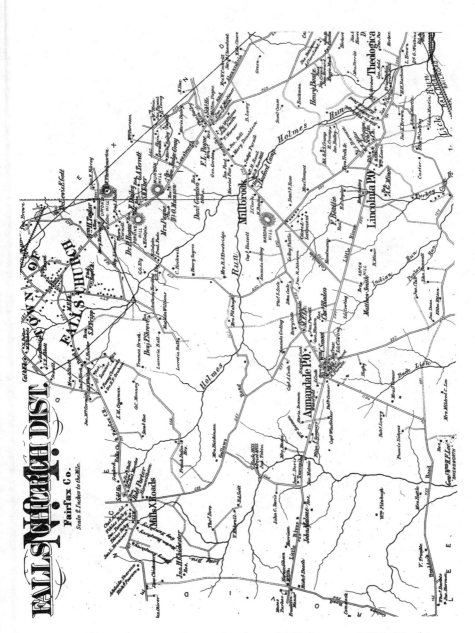

Map Section from *Atlas of 15 Miles Around Washington*, 1879, Hopkins

Photo by Richard M. Sparks, II, 1963

Old Bailey's School, 1901

Porter Studios Photo

Munson-Wilkins House, 1861-1963

Advertisement of Barnum and Bailey's Menagerie, 1897

Maury as it appeared about 1890 when it had 100 rooms
Drawing by James Montgomery

serve them meals separately and to keep their meetings as peaceable as possible.

Shortly after this, the Gordon homestead was burned by Union soldiers apparently by accident, since there had been talk of using it as officers' quarters. The family of young children moved into a hurriedly renovated barn belonging to the Birch family near Falls Church.

A Gordon cousin, David Stuart Gordon, was a recent West Point graduate in 1861. When the war broke out, he was a second lieutenant in the 2nd Dragoons on duty in Washington. Excerpts from an official military letter reveal David Gordon's special knowledge of the area which was utilized immediately after the beginning of the war:

Camp Union, Va. (Ball's Crossroads)
June 1, 1961.

> Sir:
> I left camp on eve of 31st May in command of a detachment composed of 50 men, with 2nd Lt. D.S. Gordon, 2nd Dragoons, temporarily attached, for the purpose of reconnoitering the country near Fairfax ... (Skirmishes are described briefly in the report. The War's first Confederate officer casualty, Capt. Marr, was killed during one of these skirmishes which took place near Fairfax on the early morning of June 1st.) ... *We learned the enemy's forces were to be increased to a thousand men. Lt. Gordon rendered valuable service. ...*[4]

> C. H. Thompkins
> 1st Lt., 2nd Cav.

The Munson family suffered their own share of misfortunes during the summer of 1861. Daniel and Miles Munson and brothers and sisters who may still have been living at the family home tried to keep ahead of the nursery's workload during the time their father was involved with politics. Both young Munson men experienced gunfire when caught between the lines. Many of Daniel and Miles' experiences have been preserved in the writings of their niece, Mary Virginia Fenwick Lane.

One night, probably August 24, 1861, when Confederate units were probing the Federal line, Miles had a horse shot beneath him while riding on Leesburg Pike between his home and Bailey's Crossroads. Two bullets went through his hat and his coat was riddled with balls but he was not injured himself. The dead horse when examined the next day had 14 balls in its body.

On the afternoon of August 27th, Daniel, frantic with frustration over the theft of his New York horse, Barney, by a Union soldier set out to get her back. He finally did retrieve her but on returning home, he found that his house which had been in the hands of General Richardson's Federals while they were constructing cannon emplacements had been captured by a large group of Confederates. As Daniel rode up, the Confederates, thinking he was a Union officer, fired at him. He whirled about and fled down Leesburg Pike for sanctuary at Bailey's Crossroads where he knew over 3,000 Federals were stationed. They in turn thought he was a Confederate spy. They promptly took him prisoner and packed him off to be imprisoned in the new Fairfax Episcopal Seminary tower room on Seminary Hill which had been hastily improvised as a temporary place of detention. While in his "prison in the sky," as he called it, small boys jeered up at him, saying, "They're gittin' the gallows ready for you!"

A newsboy threw in a newspaper to Daniel with the headlines:

Rebels on Munson Hill! In Sight of Washington!

Daniel tried numerous times without success to be released. Finally on the third day, General Kearney came back to his Seminary Headquarters, recognized Daniel's pass, and released him.[5] Before leaving, Daniel heard the story of how Kearney, who had lost an arm in the Mexican War, had sat in his saddle for the greater part of three days and nights vigilantly watching Munson Hill from Bailey's Crossroads. He had been trying to see what the Confederates might be planning to do in their newly gained outpost so close to Washington.

After being released, Daniel decided to ride to Bailey's before joining his family who had fled to Washington. While he was looking up the Pike toward his occupied home, General McClellan, Commanding General of the Potomac Army, rode up and observed to his aides that in his opinion Munson Hill was "heavily cannoned."[6]

Jeb Stuart's Confederates Take Munson Hill

The commanding officer of the Confederate troops which took Munson Hill on August 27, 1861, and held it for the next five weeks was Colonel Jeb Stuart. A West Point graduate, Stuart has been described as both a conscientious, capable tactician and also a show-off, full of theatrics. Stuart and his men became famous for wearing dapper uniforms, unique with their own style of scarlet lined capes and hats which featured long feathery plumes. His men adored him, especially that summer when he led thm to victories which were headlined around the world. To have reached Munson Hill within sight of Washington itself, following his victories at Bull Run, was more than enough to set a mood for jubilation! Stuart kept a banjo player on his staff, and between actions he usually permitted much gaiety.

Following is a report filed by Jeb Stuart to General Longstreet from the Munson Hill encampment.

Report of Colonel Jeb Stuart, Confederate Army
    Headquarters, Munson's HIll, August 28, 1861

General:
    I enclose a list of killed and wounded (1 killed and 6 wounded). I have no time for a detailed report of the affair of yesterday, but I acquainted Rev. D. Ball, chaplain to my regiment, as well as Major Skinner, with all the particulars, and requested them to inform you last night, which I hope will answer for the present. As soon as it was fair light this morning I had a piece of rifled cannon, Washington Battery (Artillery) brought clandestinely in position to bear on Bailey's Cross-Roads and fired four shots, distance being by the shots 1,350 yards. The shots took effect admirably, dispersing the entire force at that point, and developed what it was my object to ascertain—that they had no artillery there. Munson's Hill is a fine place for a battery, and is more capable of defense than Munson's Hill. The fire of artillery dispersed also a long line of skirmishers, who ran precipitately without being in the slightest danger from its shots. The last Regiment is at Falls Church, and I have directed its commander to hold himself in readiness to move up to my support, or act to the left, as circumstances indicate. Two companies of that regiment are ordered to occupy the ridge along Upton's. I sent back Beckham's section of artillery, as the men were pretty well used up from fatigue and hunger, and I am now going to send back to Mason's Hill Major Johnson's command (2 companies), and relieve those companies of your command here, who have been out so long, and send them back to Falls Church. I

believe this a fine line of defense; I mean the line passing through this and Mason's Hill. Every inch of the road is visible from here to Bailey's Cross-Roads. The force now here and at Falls Church I consider sufficient for the present, and the best school of practice possible for our troops. I consider the enemy's design not to meet us outside their trenches in force pretty well developed. Please send this to General Johnston for me.

Most respectfully, your obedient servant,

Jeb Stuart
Colonel Commanding

P.S. The scattered fragments of the force at Bailey's Cross-roads reassembled and I have the piece in position to stir them up again whenever they group in sufficient force to warrant the expenditure of our ammunition.[7]

Jeb Stuart received his promotion to Brigadier General at a ceremony which included numerous cavalrymen on September 24, 1861, while he was in command of Munson Hill. A Confederate historical marker lost during building operations at the site in the early 1950s commemorates this event.

Union Fortifications

The highpoint on the ridge between Bailey's Crossroads and the town of Falls Church was Taylor's Tavern. Several important roads converge and cross there today, and nestled below the ridge is a shopping center which touted itself on grand opening day in 1956 as the "world's largest ... where anything can be purchased!" One store features an activities room called the Fort Buffalo Room. Fort Buffalo was an earthwork fortification constructed during the Civil War's early months by a Federal unit believed to have been from Buffalo, New York. Brevet Major General John Barnard directed the fortification of the 34-mile periphery around Washington's bowl-like terrain, 37 miles including the local ridge. In his report on the defenses of Washington, he mentioned the importance of the headlands:

...."Four miles west of Arlington is a cluster of commanding heights, lying between Four Mile Run and a tributary of Great Hunting Creek, which form a position of a certain military importance. The point alluded to is central, nearly, to the concave line of defensive works from Chain Bridge to Great Hunting Creek.

"It was first occupied by General McDowell preparatory to his advance to attack the insurgent forces near Manassas. Soon after the retreat of his Army into Washington, it was occupied as an advanced position by the rebels. On their withdrawing therefrom, it was taken possession of and forti-fied by General McClellan, the works called Fort Ramsay, Fort Buffalo, and one on Munson's Hill.

"... These works, though always thereafter maintained, were not, properly speaking, a part of the Defenses of Washington. Under ordinary circumstances a cavalry picket, supported by a few companies of infantry, occupied the point. In case of a retreat of our forces from Virginia upon Washing-ton, the holding of this position temporarily or permanently might be of high importance should a battle be delivered in this vicinity.

"... A major line of defence was Ball's Crossroads and Fort Richardson to the South which overlooked Columbia Pike." (It was thought that if the enemy reached this low spot in the ravine, he could easily at this point be turned back.)

"... Fort Ward (near Seminary Hill) was one of the largest forts constructed up to that time. It controlled the approach to Alexandria by the interval between Hunting Creek and Four Mile Run ... The fire of its rifled guns (which included a large Parrott hundred pounder) reached the more distant eleva-tions of Munson and Mason Hills."[8]

Although the detailed maps which accompanied Barnard's report show fortifications similar in design to the recently recon-structed Fort Ward, no plans or specifications of Forts Buffalo, Ramsay, or Munson Hill were included. The Military Index in the National Archives does not indicate where the drawings may be found.

Unlike the skirmishes at Bailey's Crossroads, Fort Buffalo apparently never was attacked. General Jubal Early had made a study of local terrain for the Confederate high command in the summer of 1861; his detailed map is in the Library of Congress. Early's knowledge of Federal defensive positions and topography caused him to lead his troops, not from the south, but through Maryland to the Northern defenses at Fort Stevens when he attempted to invade Washington in 1864.

A Spy In The Sky

In late August 1861, the Federals were on the heights which were to become known as Fort Buffalo, and they were also at Camp Bailey's Crossroads. The Confederates were at Munson Hill with a small Signal detachment operating clandestinely on Upton Hill under cover of darkness to contact Southern spies in Washington. Confederate supplies could arrive only by the back road to Fairfax. Thus, the two armies began their contest for the area.

The Federals began to notice ominous looking cannon aimed at them from Munson Hill. The crown of the hill in those days was clear of dense foliage. Only Timothy Munson's peach seedlings dotted the sloping landscape toward Arlington.

Washingtonians were well-aware of these fortifications. For several weeks in late summer, a fascinating preoccupation was a trip to the unfinished Capitol dome to nervously view through binoculars the Southern sentinels, horses, and cannon on Munson Hill. The Confederate flag could be seen waving in the breeze on a very tall pole.

To get a better look on August 29th, the Federals sent aloft the famous balloonist and the country's first military aeronaut, Thaddeus Lowe, in his balloon *Union*. This was his first official aerial mission. As Lowe swayed over the area between Munson Hill and Ball's Crossroads, Lt. Thomas Rosser, commanding a section of Stuart's New Orleans Washington Artillery, fired at the balloon. The Federals quickly winched the balloon down.

Captain Alexander, who headed the Signal detachment at Upton Hill, observed the firing from his vantage point and later wrote an exultant letter to his father: "We sent shell so near old Lowe and his balloon that he came down as fast as gravity could bring him!"

Impressed by all the activity, Lowe transmitted to Union Headquarters his first official report:

"...A thousand men are erecting formidable works on Munson Hill. ..." (Intelligence which Lt. Gordon's clandestine report had predicted as far back as May 31st.)

Several balloon ascensions took place from Munson Hill during the fall of 1861. Once General McClellan himself ascended with Lowe to reconnoiter the Confederate withdrawl. Lowe's ascensions and his aerial intelligence reports marked a first along those lines.

On the night of September 13, 1861, following the Federal defeat at nearby Lewinsville, Lowe made another nighttime balloon ascension. He saw a large fire begin to flare and burn brightly on Munson HIll and at other places on the headlands. There was much cheering, and men could be seen in the flickering firelight. Other fires soon appeared with more cheering. Three cannon near a burning building were fired toward Washington and were accompanied by continued shouting. Later analyses determined this to have been Jeb Stuart and his men celebrating. Some of the buildings burned were probably outbuildings of Timothy Munson's first home, *Pendennis.*

By early September, the Confederates also had obtained a balloon and inflated it on Munson Hill's highest crest where it was seen far and wide around the countryside. For some reason it was never used. It would have been useful to reconnoiter the situation which, with approaching winter, looked bad. Furthermore, their outpost was surrounded by Federal troops, with the exception of the small back road.

In late September, Confederate forces suddenly withdrew to Fairfax and Manassas. Union Forces trod Leesburg Pike without incident to the hill where they discovered that at least some of the cannon both Lowe and McClellan had thought so formidable were "Quaker Guns."

A chagrined eyewitness account of the Quaker Guns discovery appeared in the *Washington Star:*

"...The 'fort' on Munson's Hill I find to be perhaps 300 yards long in the circuit of its parapet, the whole being nothing more than Infantry breast-works, having however a rather formidable 'Quaker Gun,' in the shape of an ash log with a dab of black paint at the butt to represent the muzzle. Such other and more valuable guns as they may have had here had been carefully removed by the Confeds when they withdrew their pickets previously. At the earth-work to the rear of Munson's Hill the retreating Confederates had left six sections of stovepipe mounted in the six embrasures, and some rather formidable looking (at a distance) earth-works upon Mason's Hill proved, on the occupation of that point by our troops, to be just about of the same bogus nature. The stars and stripes which have displaced the 'stars and bars' here, now float from a small pine tree nearly upon the apex of the hill. There is a quantity of straw on the westerly slope of the hill, but nothing to indicate that the enemy has ever been here in any force."[9]

The Grand Review

Washingtonians began stirring early on the unseasonably warm morning of the 20th day of November, 1861. Something was going to take place out at Bailey's Crossroads that no one wanted to miss. General McClellan, who had replaced the retired, elderly General Scott, was to review the troops. President Lincoln, his Presidential cabinet, and foreign dignitaries were to be there.

The restrictions on civilian travel to Bailey's were lifted for the occasion. Everyone dressed up and felt very festive. This was the way a war should be conducted! The best route for civilian travel to Bailey's, well advertised in advance in the newspapers, was over Aqueduct Bridge (now Key Bridge) past Ball's Crossroads to Munson Hill by way of the road now called Wilson Boulevard. Everyone soon discovered that the road was well-jammed with carriages. It took half a day to make the trip. For those people who made the trip perhaps 75,000 viewers, not including the 75,000 soldiers to parade, it was a day to remember.

Lincoln did not reach Munson Hill until a quarter past noon, but the troops were waiting. On his arrival, he received a salute by salvos of artillery. Cheers arose and continued until General McClellan arrived with his staff and 1800 regular cavalry to begin the review. The General, followed by President Lincoln and Secretaries Seward and Cameron, set their mounts at a fast pace and galloped to the reviewing stand past immense bodies of infantry, cavalry, and artillery which extended for miles in the fields between Munson Hill and Bailey's Crossroads and even beyond.

The day before, some of the troops had been ordered to construct a reviewing stand from fences torn down in the fields. The structure was rather imposing as it stood on a small rise in the ground midway between Munson Hill and Bailey's Crossroads. From the stand Lincoln watched the troops slosh through the muddy fields in brilliant formation from the Crossroads toward the hill.

All was pageantry! All was gaiety! The soldiers sang as they marched. One of the favorites adopted by some of the regiments and sung over and over was "John Brown's Body." This was one of the largest bodies of troops ever reviewed. Each soldier passed before the President and General McClellan in full battle equipment, each man supplied with 40 rounds of cartridges.

Each division was accompanied by ambulances so that every branch of the Army might be represented. Fifty regimental bands marched in the gleaming sunshine with colors flying high amid the flourish of trumpets and the cheers of the throng.

The *New York Daily Tribune* reporter gave this description: "The Great Review at Bailey's Crossroads was a very remarkable spectacle. Apart from the effect upon those not accustomed to such displays, it is declared by Officers long used to foreign service, that few demonstrations in Europe have exceeded this one in precision, regularity, and evidence of rapid soldierly development. ... The feat (was) no ordinary achievement!"

Mine Eyes Have Seen The Glory

Mariah Bailey had to start this day early too. The President and his official party were to eat at the Crossroads Inn, and there was much to be done and no time to think about the fences being torn down.

The beautiful pond was being drained by soldiers for the fish which were needed for food. The weather had turned windy, and the plan to feed the increasing multitude outdoors would have to be abandoned. Mariah realized the inn's interior would not be nearly large enough to hold the numbers of spectators looking for food and warmth.

Luckily, Mariah remembered the old circus tent as a place to shelter and feed the crowd coming from the grand review. She gathered her sons and some of the soldiers and directed their efforts to assemble the tent. When the tent was successfully erected, it had a splendid setting in the gardens on the grounds of *Maury*.

The President and Mrs. Lincoln, whose demeanor that day impressed everybody most favorably, and the others were fed. For everybody it remained the festive occasion it had started out to be.

The exuberant crowds felt the extra exhilaration of knowing the event would appear pictorially in *Harpers* and other publications. Youthful artists at work sketching the paraders were perched atop the big barn near the Crossroads.

The French Comte de Paris, Prince de Joinville, third son of Louis Phillippe, was also present. No one realized he experienced great "curiosity" (as he later put it to his countrymen) over "civilians boldly caracoling at the head of a brilliant military cortege." It would not have mattered if he had expressed his opinion because nothing could spoil that day of jubilee, pomp, and pageantry, not even a military skirmish.

An excursion by a small detachment of Confederate troops, probably sent to reconnoiter Federal strength with field glasses in the woods behind Munson Hill was halted by Union troops detached from the parade route. This action sent a shiver down the spines of spectators at Munson Hill. In the midst of the revelry they became somber witnesses to the omen of bloody battles yet to be fought between the opposing armies.

At Bailey's Crossroads, the marching and singing continued until well past dark. Washingtonians began to return home only to get tied up in the worst traffic snarl of the 19th century. Newspaper accounts do not indicate that Lincoln elected to stay, but the Bailey family maintains that he did. It would seem without helicopter or interstate highway, he would have sensibly stayed the night at the inn.

Julia Ward Howe's Story

Another witness to the pageantry of the grand review at Munson Hill was Julia Ward Howe who had visited the Munsons with Governor and Mrs. Andrews of New Jersey, the Reverend Mr. Clarke, and other friends. Her husband, Samuel Howe, temporarily working in Washington, had recently been appointed to help form the Sanitary Commission which was to function in behalf of soldiers' welfare.

She had been one of the witnesses of the enemy action at Munson Hill that day, and on her return trip to her room at the Willard Hotel, she felt despondency mixed with exhilaration over the parade and music. She could not know that out of these events would come the song, "Battle Hymn of the Republic," which, over one hundred years later, is cherished as a truly great American anthem. Its words are well known: "I have seen Him in the watchfires of a hundred circling camps ... His truth is marching on! Glory Hallelujah!"

The following description of Julia Howe's activities the night she returned to the Willard Hotel is taken from her autobiography:

"As this ofttold tale about the circumstances under which I wrote 'Battle Hymn of the Republic' has no unimportant part in the story of my life, I will briefly add it to these records..."

"... I distinctly remember that a feeling of discouragement came over me as I drew near the city of Washington. I thought of the women of my acquaintance whose sons or husbands were fighting our great battle; the women themselves serving in the hospital or busying themselves with work of the sanitary mission.

"My husband was beyond the age of military service, my eldest son was but a stripling; my youngest was a child of not more than two years. I would not leave my nursery to follow the march of our armies. Neither had I the practical deftness which the preparing and packing of sanitary stores demanded.

"Something seemed to say to me, 'You would be glad to serve, but you cannot help anyone; you have nothing to give, and there is nothing for you to do!'

"Yet, because of my sincere desire, a word was given me to say which did strengthen the hearts of those who fought in the field and of those who languished in the prison.

"We were invited one day to attend a review of troops at some distance from town. While we were engaged in watching the maneuvers, a sudden movement of the enemy necessitated enemy action. The review was discontinued, and we saw a detachment of soldiers gallop to the assistance of a small body of our men who were in imminent danger of being surrounded and cut off from retreat. The regiments remaining on the field were ordered to march to their cantonments. We returned to the city very slowly, of necessity for the troops nearly filled the road. My dear minister was in the carriage with me, as were several other friends. To beguile the rather tedious drive, we sang from time to time snatches of the Army songs so popular at that time, concluding with 'John Brown's Body.'

"The soldiers seemed to like this, and answered back, 'Good for you!'

"Mr. Clarke said, 'Mrs. Howe, why do you not write some good words for that stirring tune?'

"I replied that I had often wished to do this, but had not as yet found in my mind any leading toward it.

"I went to bed that night as usual, and slept, according to my wont, quite soundly. I awoke in the gray of the morning twilight, and, as I lay waiting for the dawn, the long lines of the desired poem began to twine themselves in mind.

"Having thought out all the stanzas, I said to myself, 'I must get up and write these verses down, lest I fall asleep again and forget them.' So, with a sudden effort, I sprang out of bed, and found in the dimness an old stump of a pen which I remembered to have used the day before. I scrawled the verses almost without looking at the paper. I had learned to do this when on previous occasions attacks of 'versification' had visited me in the night, and I feared to have recourse to a light lest I should awake the baby, who slept near me. I was always obliged to decipher my scrawl before another night should intervene, as it was only legible while the matter was fresh in my mind.

"At this time, having completed my writing, I returned to bed and fell asleep, saying to myself, 'I like this better than most things I have written!'"

CHAPTER FIVE

Bleak Days

Nobody escaped hardship through the years of the war. Farms fell into disrepair. The North thought of local citizens as rebels because they were Virginians, but if one ventured into Washington to sell produce or obtain supplies, he might find himself branded by Southern neighbors as a conveyor of military information to the Yankees. Local men whose property was being used by troops for training were declared exempt from military service. The Bailey and Munson men were included in this arrangement which left many suspicious draft-age men in the area.

In August 1861, during skirmishing, *Maury*'s walls were punctured more than once by artillery shells. At one point shortly after Stuart's capture of Munson Hill, the Federals practiced their own brand of Quaker Gun warfare in an effort to intimidate. They hurriedly constructed imposing cannon made of stovepipes placed between sets of wagonwheels and placed them in prominent positions beside the blacksmith shop.

During the following engagement, Jeb Stuart's rifled cannon cut loose with such a shelling that *Maury,* caught in the line of fire, was in danger of being wrecked. Worse yet, Mariah Bailey and some of her younger boys were huddled with the Barcrofts and others for protection inside. Through the fusillade, Lewis Bailey fled to plead with Union officers to move their fake guns elsewhere so *Maury* could survive. The officers cooperated because they too had plans for *Maury*'s future as an officers' quarters and mess. Also, the Crossroads Inn was to be used for a while as a headquarters.

During this same time period, the colorful but rowdy Garibaldi Regiment bivouacked at Baileys. They and detachments of Michiganders and other units often passed out of formation through local fields and yards helping themselves to anything they wanted. While Stuart's troops were at Munson's, citizens were permitted to cross military lines to visit neighbors by tying a white cloth to a stick and carrying it, knees trembling, fearful that some trigger-happy soldier might be looking down the barrel of a gun at them.

After Stuart's retreat, the New York 37th regiment marched .*en masse* to occupy Munson Hill. When the Munson family returned, they found the house and furnishings to have been greatly damaged. The youngest daughter, Lucy Munson, could see numerous "poetic notes, embellished with artistic efforts" addressed to her on the walls by beaux who were with Stuart. All their table covers were missing. Someone told them later that some of the men had cut holes in them and draped them over their shoulders in imitation of Jeb Stuart's cape. For Lucy Munson the worst blow of all was the disappearance of all her bonnets with the departing cavalrymen. These, in the style of the time, had been prettily adorned with long, feathery ostrich plumes.

Stuart's Union replacement, the New York 37th regiment, soon acquired a reputation as thieves and vandals. Livestock and outbuildings were destroyed; chickens, corn, and fruit were consumed; much personal property was stolen or burned. These acts made the theft by Stuart's men of tablecloths and bonnet feathers small by comparison. Children and young women were soon sent elsewhere and several members of the Union military were court-martialed for offenses committed while stationed in the area. The appellation, "Damnyankee," came into use during October 1861 by citizens regardless of whether they were Secessionist or Unionist in sentiment.

The Terrett family home, *Oakwood,* was destroyed and the family had to find new quarters. *Church Hill House* was commandeered for a while and used as a field hospital following the first battle at Manassas. Casualties were buried nearby. (A military cemetery is believed to be under the J. E. B. Stuart High School athletic field.) Dr. Barcroft and his family moved into the Bailey home when their house at *Millbrook* was burned to the ground and the mill made inoperable by Federals retreating from Manassas.

Major Mosby Tries To Capture Timothy Munson

Special passes were issued by the U. S. War Department to certain citizens of the South who were thereby authorized to enter Washington across the Potomac River bridges. Timothy Munson used his pass freely and as the months of the war went by, he was full of talk and plans for a new state that might be created out of western Virginia. Through nursery-business dealings in past times with people to the west, he knew many of them very well; he knew that they did not want to be part of the disunion of America.

Munson belonged to the knowledgeable group who felt that if western Virginia formed a new state, Lincoln's re-election would be certain and there would be no further toying with the idea of compromise with the South. As hardships for the North increased, a belief that Confederate and Federal Governments could co-exist gained in popularity. Munson firmly voiced his opinion as being the same as Lincoln's, that is, that the struggle should continue until reunification of the United States was achieved.

Munson's biographer indicated that, at some time during the war, Munson felt a need for a secret hideaway. He fashioned two or three in the nursery just in case Southern guerrillas might come through Federa lines to capture him. He hoped he would never have to run out into the night and hide as his health was not good.

These fears were not without reason. In February 1863, Confederate John Mosby was given command of partisan rangers and attached to General Jeb Stuart's Command. His directive was to "operate in clandestine manner behind the enemy's lines."

Major Mosby's men adopted the plumed hat and cape of the Stuart uniform, and they soon became famous for their startling departures from orthodox cavalry warfare. Mosby's guerrillas were active throughout Northern Virginia. Their activities were the talk of Washington.

On numerous occasions, Mosby raiders surprised Union units throughout Northern Virginia. One night in the early fall of 1863, Timothy Munson was indeed Major Mosby's "target for tonight," just as he had feared.

Miles Munson's diary gives the following account of that night:

"A party of guerrillas, about 40 in number, under cover of darkness and by unfrequented paths, made their way through the Union lines, and surrounded my father's house about midnight after the family had retired to rest. The purpose was to capture my father. My sister Lucy with quick woman's wit devised a plan to throw them off the track. My brother Daniel had been sick in bed for a week, and under the doctor's care. My father was in bed in a room adjoining the parlor where the guerrillas were assembled. That door of his room was partly open, and for some unaccountable reason that room was overlooked in the hasty search. The guerilla chief said to my sister that he desired to see Mr. Munson; she replied, 'He is upstairs, sick in bed.'

"He directed a surgeon belonging to his party to examine the sick man and report whether he could be removed or not. He soon reported in the affirmative. In the meantime, some of the party, who had remained outside, collected all the horses of any value, five in number, and having assisted my brother to mount one of them, they all left the premises.

"When near Falls Church, about 2 miles distant Mosby, who was riding by the side of my brother, remarked, 'Mr. Munson, I supposed you to be a much older man.' "My brother replied, 'I suppose your object was to capture my father, and you have taken me by mistake.' "When about 7 miles from my father's, they ran into a strong Union picket force who received them with a volley. Mosby gave the command for each one to look out for himself. In the confusion my brother got separated from the command and escaped. He passed the remainder of the night in the woods, and reached home by circuitous route next day."[1]

Mr. Munson Lane, the great nephew of both Daniel and Miles Munson, recalls hearing that because his Uncle Daniel had been so ill with typhoid fever at the time of his capture, he could only cling weakly, hands clasped around his beloved horse's neck. It was old Barney, navigating on her own, who brought Daniel all seven miles of the way home to Munson Hill.

Lucy Munsun Visits President Lincoln

In spite of Timothy Munson's prominence, times were hard. The Munson family needed money for living expenses; the nursery business was on hold throughout much of the war. At one point in 1861, Lucy Munson borrowed a bonnet and headed for Washington. She had heard there were government jobs for women. Feeling daring and yet patriotic, she determined to see President Lincoln. She and one of her brothers, whom she had no doubt sworn to secrecy, rode in the carriage driven by the Munson carriage man whose descendant, Mr. Herbert Smith, still lives in Arlington.

Lucy and her brother talked with Mr. Lincoln at the White House. They discussed the hardships which had befallen the people of Northern Virginia. Although in months to come Lincoln would have much praise for women's part in the war effort, he no doubt was concerned that Mr. Munson's daughter had to seek work in war-frenzied Washington. Nevertheless, he wrote a note for her, giving his personal recommendation to the Secretary of the Treasury. It was written on Executive Mansion stationery and signed with the familiar signature, "A Lincoln." This handwritten letter of Lincoln's is in the possession of Lucy Munson's great nephew, Mr. Munson Lane of Arlington.

> EXECUTIVE MANSION
> Dec 13,1861

Hon Sec of Treasury
  My Dear Sir:

I am very anxious that some employment shall be found for the young lady, bearer of this—Please see her & her brother, who are driven out from Munson's Hill.

> Yours truly
> A Lincoln

The Bailey Family Endures the War

Lewis and Mariah Bailey and several sons, including Ray and Horace, had frequently obtained special passes for travel into Washington. A typical citizen's pass read:

U. S. WAR DEPARTMENT Citizens Pass # 2649

Name:	Lewis Bailey & Team
Where:	Wash. & Alex. Baileys X Rds
Date:	Oct. 23, 1863
Duration:	expires Nov. 1, 1863
Travel reason:	to get supplies

Neighbors' suspicions were the price paid by citizens for regular travel between Virginia and Washington. Stories of espionage and civilian clandestine activities were rife throughout the war. As early as July 1861, the *Daily Picayune* reported:

"The enemy has an immense number of spies in their employ. $100,000 is said to have been spent in this way...."[2]

Lewis and Mariah, brought up in the North, could find no suitable stance to accommodate the position in which they found themselves. Few precincts in Fairfax County voted more solidly for secession than those around Bailey's Crossroads. Lewis, Dr. Barcroft, and the Unionist Timothy Munson did not vote. Probably many others, both for and against secession, stayed away from the polls in this uneasy frontier between North and South.

In February 1863, Lewis was approached by an agent of J. B. Mier, Quartermaster Contractor, who inquired about the timber on Bailey property bordering Long Branch. Lewis was told it was needed for military hospitals, and he and Mariah readily gave their agreement. Apparently, a verbal agreement on payment was made. Woodcutters under foreman John Mortimer spent weeks cutting trees which they sent to a nearby sawmill to be cut into lumber.

In October 1865, Mariah, signing Lewis' name, wrote to General M. C. Meigs, QM Department, enclosing affidavits and asking reimbursement for 894 cords of wood obtained from Bailey property. Her letter set off a legal investigation into the case. Disposition resulted from the following letter:

HQ Dept Washington
Office of Chief QM
Washington, D.C.
January 15, 1866

Brevet Major General M. C. Meigs
Quartermaster General U. S. A.

General: I have the honor to acknowledge receipt of communication from your office of the 20th ultimo requesting certain information in the case of Lewis Bailey who claims payment for wood cut on his farm in Virginia by Messrs Gilbert and Mier, contractors with Lt. Col. E. M. Greene, late Chief QM, and I beg leave to report that the only recorded evidence in this office of wood having been cut is a press copy of "List of names and property of supposed disloyal persons, from whose lands wood is now being cut for the use of the troops, hospitals and other buildings for the defences of Washington" dated "Feb. 5, 1863" which appears to have been transmitted on that day to Hon. E. M. Stanton, Sec. of War and which contains among other names that of "L. Bailey."

(s) M. Ludington
Col. and Chief QM Dept.
Washington

An indorsement of this letter vetoed payment for the wood on the basis of "disloyalty to the Federal Union."[3]

In 1878, after Lewis's death, Mariah Bailey again applied for remuneration for her property's use by Federal troops. She forwarded affidavits attesting to the loyalty of Lewis to the Union States. Her claim was accepted and some reparation was made for damages.[4]

Dear Folks, We're Coming Home

The wanderings and clashes of armies left over 618,000 men dead by injury or disease. The nation's bloodletting which had begun with taunt and potshot at Ft. Sumter, finally ended with the Southern surrender at Appomattox in April 1865. Lee's armies dispersed, and Grant and Sherman's armies tramped back for final bivouacs outside Washington in Northern Virginia.

Camp Bailey's Crossroads was the destination for many units. Tents were spread all across the fields again, two men to a tent, from Carlyn Springs to Holmes Run, from Fort Buffalo to the grounds of the Seminary. They remained here until getting separation papers or regimental orders to return to their points of origin.

It was mainly from Camp Bailey's via Columbia Pike that the great military marches up Pennsylvania Avenue originated. These went on by day and night for weeks. The parades had begun with the victory in April and continued even throughout the period of mourning for the assassinated Lincoln.

The following letters were written by William Robinson, a soldier at Camp Bailey's in those final days. Sometimes he wrote of sights to be seen in Washington. He mentioned deaths of comrades .... and trophies to be shared with homefolk ... and griping.

U. S. Christian Commission

Camp Baileys X Roads
May 25, 1865

Dear Wife,

I received your welcome letter and was glad to hear from you and that you and Willie was well. I was very much alarmed when I read the news of the dispatch Mother had received but was glad that it was another person. The Army of the Potomac left for Washington this morning for a Grand Review. They will have to march about 16 or 18 miles before they are done. Sherman's Army arrived here on Friday. Jim was down to Sherman's review on yesterday. He saw a great many of the sights in Washington. When he got back he was very tired. I would have been down but the Captain took an attack of Cramp Cholic the night before and I had to take him to the hospital in the morning and I staied with him till noon so I could not get down. At the hospital while I was down there, a lady came to see her husband that she heard was sick and the steward told her he died two days before. Em, I felt in my heart for her.

Em, I had one of the incidents of war before me today. A man in our company by the name of Sutten died on the march. And his family heard about it. His brother came to inquire for him and we could tell him nothing about him any more than that he fell behind in the march. We found out from him that his brother had been found by Sherman's Army. When they came along he was then insensible. They took him to their hospital and he died in a short time. They then wrote home to his family and that was the way we found out he was dead.

We got orders since I commenced to write this letter to make out the muster out rolls for the regiment but I don't know what it will amount to but I hope I will get home before long as I want to see you and Willie so much and never to go away from you again. The Christian Com are in camp and they gave us some pickles and dried apples the other day which was quite a luxury. I went up this morning and got a bottle of cramp medicine from them which was the very thing I wanted. Em, the Sanitary Com is a humbug. The Officers get the benefit of it and live high off it, but don't tell Brown's anything like that for they would way it was not so.

Em, enclosed you will find pieces of 3 battle flags. The plain blue is a piece of the 110th, our regiment. The one with the star is Kilpatricks, the great Cavalry Genl, the red one is a piece of the 115th battle flag. Keep them til I come home. Em, this is a bright shiny day and it is so lonesome almost everyone away from camp which makes me wish the more to be with you. Your affectionate husband.

W. H. Robinson

...Sometimes in Camp Bailey's they celebrated victory with spectacular illuminations.

Camp Baileys X Roads
May 27, 1865

Dear Wife,

I received your welcome letter yesterday evening and was glad to hear from you. Em, I feel disappointed when I don't get a letter every evenings mail. Em, we had a grand illumination in the fifth and second corps the night before last. It was a magnificent sight. You could see the lights of the fires and rockets for miles around. Just imagine 75 or 80,000 men with torches in their hands and you may have an idea what it was like. They make the rockets out of wet powder and fire them out their guns which make them go a great deal higher than any rockets you ever saw.

After the Illumination the different bands broke forth in sweet tones of music. When they played Home Sweet Home, it carried my thoughts back to my own happy hours with you and our little darling enjoying the comforts of home. But it was all imagination for when the band ceased playing I found myself cooped up in a little four by six tent shivering with cold. When I say cold I will just let you know that it has been very disagreeable weather here for a week raining and very cold all the time. With these few lines I will close. Kiss Willie for me, love to Mother and Mrs. Brown and all my friends from your affectionate husband.

W. H. Robinson

Be particular in direction to "Co G. 110 Regt Penna Vol 3rd divis 1st Brigad 2nd Army Corps Washington D.C. as there is a person of my name in another Company.

... Mostly there were the frustrations of camp life, and a longing
to be at home done with the war.

Camp Baileys X Roads
May 28, 1865

Dear Em,

This is a clear sabbeth day and I thought I could do worse
than sit down and write to you and Willie. Yesterday was
Willie's birthday and I thought about how I would like to be with
him and have him on my knee. I was looking at his picture and
could see the little dear laughing in my face as he would have
hold of my whiskers. Em, I have never received your picture
yet and have been looking very anxious for it every day but I
have been disappointed. Em, I want you to send it to me.

Em, it is a great place in the Army for playing jokes on each
other, but Jim and I had a rather severe joke played on us last
night. Some one came into our tent and stole all our rations.
We had 5 days rations of beans, 2 days rations of meat, 3 days
rations of sugar and loaves of bread. But the thieves had no
conscience. They made a clean deal of everything so we took
a light breakfast. They left us a few dried apples (I guess they
thought we could eat and drink water and swell up till we got
more rations). But I think I will make up for our loss tonight off
some one else...

Em, if a fellow wants to get out of the service now all he has
to do is to go to the hospital one day and the next day an order
will come in to make out his discharge. But I dont want to get
out that way. I want an honorable discharge from the regiment
when I come home, and I dont think that will be too long. John
Sweenys regiment will start home this week. I saw him yesterday. He was well. My love to all, good bye, kiss Willie, your
affectionate husband.

W. H. Robinson

Em, send some more stamps.[5]

CHAPTER SIX

Times of Change

After the war, the States were reunited, slaves were emancipated, and military units were mustered out. Soldiers, including Charlie and George Gordon, returned home. There was no going back to things as they were. For most of the South, the misery of the war had turned into the misery of reconstruction with scalawag and carpetbagger. For Northern Virginia like much of the war-torn nation, it was time to begin again.

When Timothy Munson died in 1867 at the age of 62, evidence of devastation was still to be seen. The U. S. Government had paid damages to the Munsons for property use and Daniel, inheriting the house and nursery, undertook restoration. In 1868 he married his Virginia sweetheart, Ruhamah Bittinger. Their child, Mary Jasper, was born in 1871 in the family home across from *Pendennis.*

When Timothy Munson first came to his hill in the early 19th century, he had done a great deal of experimentation to enrich the soil. He had gone to Alexandria and ordered quantities of Potomac and Chesapeake shad with which he fertilized the land. A few months later, he decided that the soil basically lacked lime, so he ordered ground-up oyster shells which he directed to be scattered about. He kept a large flock of sheep roaming to close-crop the grass and weeds. Nearby farm and circus animal manure was plentiful, and during the war he sent men to Army Cavalry stables for fertilizer. These ministrations paid off handsomely, especially in the quality of his numerous peach trees.

Daniel Munson learned much from his father and in 1883 was able to write of himself: "I am very busy, having from 20 to 30 men to attend in my nursery and also 40 agents to look after..."

Daniel was described as "...a mighty successful horticulturist, having business relations from Maine to Texas. He is a deacon of the Presbyterian Church and is quite prominent in various good works." In later years, neighbors who knew about his harrowing war experiences respectfully and affectionately bestowed on him the honorary title, "Colonel."

The goverment, while beautifying Washington's Federal grounds, purchased maple trees and other species from the Munson nursery. Falls Church township planted Munson maples making the town an annual riot of color until the streets were widened in the 1940s.

Some Civil War scars did not heal so easily. Many churches of the South elected to withdraw from the governing bodies of their Northern counterpart. Most local families affiliated with Southern churches. Northern and Southern jurisdictions of several denominations overlap today in the local area.

Some acts of war, if not forgotten, were forgiven. A granddaughter of Timothy Munson, Virginia Munson. daughter of Miles, married Dr. Henry Clay Corbett. In 1910, the family rented Dr. Corbett's deceased father's house on Columbia Pike and Walter Reed Drive, Arlington, to Colonel John Singleton Mosby who had become a diplomat in the U.S. State Department. Mosby, then an old man, rented the house for three years. He was a neighbor of several Munson and Bailey families.

Another Munson descendant, Lucy Munson, married the Reverend Mr. A. A. Taylor, minister of Georgetown Presbyterian Church, who later became President of Wooster College, Ohio. Many other descendants of Timothy Munson live in Fairfax County today, including families named Munson, Lane, Corbett, DeLashmutt, and Fenwick. The Munson homestead was occupied from 1945 through 1961 by the Donald Wilkins family Completed in 1860, the Munson home was demolished in 1963 for a new landmark, Munson Hill's twelve-story apartment.

In mid-20th century Fairfax County, there are still traces to be found of the Civil War. Because Federal troops had set fire to Fairfax Court House, many early records are missing. Displayed over the records shelf in the Court House is the following typed note, defaced by handwritten comments:

> The following records of Fairfax County... listed... are not available because they were destroyed by fire during the Civil War.

The Circus

The opening of Civil War hostilities caught portions of the Zoological Institute circuses already on tour. For decades, favored wagon show trails had been Little River Turnpike and Leesburg Turnpike to Shenandoah Valley via mountain gaps. The war disrupted the local area's routine of seasonal visits by circuses. During the war, fewer than a dozen wagon shows went on tour. One of these shows was the circus of George F. Bailey, Lewis Bailey's cousin. The George F. Bailey Circus had developed from the old Aaron Turner show. Several of his shows toured back and forth to Union-sympathizing East Tennessee on the Valley Road where Stonewall Jackson's army also marched. A show would have been a welcome relief from the war, although speculation can be made that it was used (perhaps unknown to circus personnel) as a Trojan Horse for clandestine activities.

The upkeep of circus menageries had become a luxury that Hachaliah Bailey's descendants, divided by the war, found difficult to maintain. The remaining animals, trained horses, and other animals, had been taken on the circus circuit after the war by George F. Bailey and descendants of other circus families.

George F. Bailey had become a full partner in the Zoological Institute. For over fifty years this circus combine had imported, leased, and sold animals; managed circuses and menageries; loaned money, foreclosed, and in general controlled the sale and purchase of many of the animals and other circus equipment in America.

Other circusmen, giving the partners a back-handed compliment for business acumen, called them the "flatfoots," probably derived from the old saying, "I will put my foot down flat, and will, or will not, do this or that!"

After the Civil War, Phineas T. Barnum, almost 60 and rich from Jennie Lind's concerts and his wartime exhibits of Tom Thumb, began accumulating interesting shows and circuses from tired and war-exhausted people. He spent several years touring the west and war-torn South, culminating the tour with a stop-off at Washington, D.C.

Lewis Bailey died in 1870. Barnum probably heard the news of the death of his old benefactor's son when he visited Washington in the early 1870s. Some believe he visited the local Bailey family during this period. It is known that the George F. Bailey Circus and other shows of the Zoological Institute were acquired some time in the 1870s by Barnum, who thus became no longer the agent but the sole owner.

Barnum, forerunner of modern press-agentry, assembled all his newly acquired exhibits and circuses, and upon buying the George F. Bailey Circus in 1875, dubbed it The Greatest Show On Earth!

George F. Bailey continued to act as one of Barnum's managers until he retired, a rich man, in late 1880. He traveled about the world for a number of years but kept his residence in New York City where he died February 20, 1903.

The Greatest Show on Earth

In 1881 the local Bailey family heard the news of the final merger of Barnum with the last of the Bailey Circuses. Mariah's brother-in-law, Fred Bailey, an agent for many years with the Zoological Institute's Robinson Circus, had taken an interest in an intelligent young orphan named Jim McGinnis who had run away to join the circus. Jim, who became a Union supplier in the Civil War, took the name Bailey. After the war, James Bailey assembled a large circus under the banner of Cooper, Bailey, and Hutchinson. It included the Great London Circus, Sanger's Royal British Menagerie, and the Grand International Allied Shows. This circus was approached by Barnum to combine with his own "greatest show." This final merging of the Barnum and Bailey Circuses took place in Wilmington. Delaware.

Barnum became more and more involved with building up a circus of tremendous proportions. Further merging with the famous Ringling Brothers Circus and Forepaugh Circus enabled Barnum's dream of a truly gigantic circus to come true.[2]

James Bailey managed the circus when it was on tour. During a tour of Europe in the late 19th century, the German Kaiser admired the immensity of this circus and its logistical arrangements. As a result, German military observers were assigned to travel with the circus while it was in Europe. Later, American military observers also traveled with Barnum and Bailey's for the same reason.

The Greatest Show On Earth was the first of the modern-day circuses with amazing exhibits and three-ring acts. Barnum and another manager, W. C. Coup, noting that receipts were greatest when the circus played metropolitan areas, decided to put the entire circus on the railroad. Afterwards, they played only in cities. The era of Hachaliah Bailey's circus associates from early wagon days was at an end, and Bailey's Crossroads at its junction of turnpikes was no longer needed for wintering quarters.

Sarasota, Florida, became the great new wintering grounds for the huge aggregation of animals and equipment. Some of the land from this circus property was reserved for the building of New College, Sarasota. The college library has become the repository for much of America's fund of circus lore and scattered records. Other repositories are the Circus Hall of Fame, Sarasota; the Hertzberg Circus Collection, San Antonio, Texas Public Library; and Somers Circus Museum in the Somers, New York, Town House formerly the Elephant Hotel.

Carrie Brown Rorer of Philadelphia, Pennsylvania, and Somers, New York, is related to several of the circus families who were involved in the Zoological Institute. One relative, Benjamin Brown, was the early explorer and collector of animals for the circuses of his relative, Hachaliah Bailey, and associates. Her great grandfather was Dr. John Woolverington Barcroft, for whom Lake Barcroft, Virginia, was named when Alexandria Reservoir was developed in 1950 as a residential area. Mrs. Rorer is Curator of Somers Historical Museum which is maintained in the Somers Town House. A descendant of the Baileys, Browns, and Barcrofts, she has attracted nationwide attention through lectures on the early American circus.

Although it is Phineas T. Barnum who is best remembered as the circus impresario, and indeed he was the greatest, but it was Hachaliah Bailey who inspired his career. It was the several Bailey circuses which formed the nucleus for the ever-to-be-remembered Greatest Show on Earth. In a final twist, after years under various ownership, the corporate headquarters for The Greatest Show on Earth, Ringling Brothers and Barnum & Bailey Circus, has returned to the area and has its main office across the Potomac in Washington, D.C.

The House With A Hundred Rooms

When Lewis Bailey died in 1870, Mariah had the Crossroads Inn moved to *Maury* and fashioned into two long wings for the old mansion. This combination gave the locally fabled house a grand total of 100 rooms.

Maury became a popular boarding home attracting many Washington families and guests of the Willard Hotel who would come to the countryside to spend a weekend or the summer. Guests who enjoyed riding to hounds found Virginia hunters in the stable. Many equestrians headed for the old circular riding ring. The Baileys also kept Morgans for driving and Percherons for farm work.

The hundred-room house could be seen through the trees from Leesburg Pike not far from a newer house built about 1880 as a wedding gift for Horace Bailey and bride. *Maury's* front facade faced squarely toward Cherry Lane now called Moray Lane which extends from Durbin Place to Columbia Pike within a hundred yards of the Crossroads. A 1930 magazine article described *Maury* this way:

> "There is still evidence that this age-worn place was a veritable Eden in bygone days. . . Part of the old mansion is now in ruins, but the main body of it is still in liveable condition. Typical of early American homes, a big hall runs through the center of it, and on one side of the hall is a spacious dining room and kitchen. In the dining room there is still evidence of the manner in which food was protected from flying insects. For when Mrs. Bailey served meals, a servant was stationed in the cellar to pull the cord which set in motion a number of fans attached to the ceiling of the dining room. . ."

The silks and satin gowns of Mariah's youthful indulgences were stored in trunks in some of *Maury's* rooms. As a girl, she lived for a while in the home of her Grandfather Green, a military officer and relative of the influential Green family of colonial New England. Mariah's granddaughters remember pleasurable hours of preening in their grandmother's numerous old costumes and vying for the feather fans, gold-pendant earrings, and fingerless golves.

In spite of improvements after the Civil War, *Maury* never recovered its past grandeur. Fires plagued the place, perhaps because hay was stored for several seasons in unused rooms in the old inn wing after Mariah's death.

Mariah's later years were bedredden; her hip was broken in a fall while on an errand about her estate. She was reluctant to relinquish management of the property to her sons who were operating their own businesses in the 1890s. They apparently lost much of the incentive to continue in the communal, family-centered enterprises envisioned by Hachaliah and Lewis Bailey.

Granddaughters recall Mariah as a delicate little lady, her energetic mind concerned mainly with business matters. Her granddaughters often peeked in at Grandma's sickbed. Her doorway was guarded by two trained lean greyhounds who permitted only those they knew to enter the room.

Mariah's bedside companion was a South American parrot presented to her by circus officials when they heard she had been injured. Poll's vocabulary was a shocking jargon of Spanish and circusese. He also quickly picked up local names. It amused Mariah to have Poll call from her bedroom window to family members who might be walking about *Maury's* grounds. Poll, the hounds, servants, friends, and most of her large family were with Mariah when she died after several years' illness in 1896.

After Mariah's death, taxes and other expenses caused considerable Bailey land to be sold. Luther Payne of Fauquier County, antecedent of the present Crossroads family, purchased about seventy acres of Bailey land, the first of his extensive land acquisitions. His stone house built on the site of the old inn is a mid-20th century landmark. *Maury* was sold as a summer home to J. Millard Moore of Washington. It was allowed to deteriorate and in the 1930s was called the "haunted house" by local children. Before *Maury* was accidentally burned to the ground on the night of December 19, 1943, a portion of the wing-addition and other buildings were moved. This house was bought and occupied by the Charles Miller family and is now used as Fairfax Brewster Private School.

CHAPTER SEVEN

Epilogue

A local real estate boom had been long anticipated by speculators in 1790 when the site of the Federal City was selected. However, the price paid in that era, $7 to $25 an acre, prevailed throughout the years until the 20th century. In 1900, the population of Bailey's Crossroads was only 95 persons. The price rise finally did come after World War II. At that time the most pressing questions for most people were, "Where shall we work?" and "Where shall we live?" For many, after selecting Washington, the last question was narrowed down to "which house and which lot?"

Now prices have continued to skyrocket. In 1982, the average value of a single family dwelling (usually on a quarter-acre lot) in Fairfax County was determined by the County's Office of Research and Statistics to be $120,825.00. In 1985 when a newcomer looks for a place to live, he is astonished at housing's high cost. While there are some older houses on small lots dating from the 1950s, most new residents are priced out of the "in-close" single family home, and must limit their decision to "which condo on which floor of whatever highrise is affordable," or "how far outside the Beltway can we realistically commute from?"

The historic old courthouse in Fairfax City that once was adequate as the seat of county government now lies in the shadow of the nine-story Massey Building which itself is only the largest of a constellation of new buildings put up to handle the burgeoning increase in functions and responsibilities. Retail businesses and services cluster along Northern Virginia's highways throughout the region. Massive shopping centers such as those at Tyson's Corners, Seven Corners, Springfield, and Fair Oaks Malls are jammed day and night with shoppers.

Fairfax County has become a part of Greater Washington. With its network of interlocking highways, it is connected directly with the District of Columbia. Historic communities have merged into one giant megapolis. Tyson's Corner, the site of Fairfax County's first courthouse in the 18th century, has become a major shopping and business area. Annandale and Seven Corners, remembered in legend as 17th century fur-trading centers between Indians and Europeans, are major shopping and residential areas. Falls Church, Munson Hill, Ball's Crossroads, and dozens of other small communities have merged into the continuous Arlington-Fairfax bedroom community serving the nation's capital.

Bailey's Crossroads which was formed in 1809 by the crossing of Columbia Pike with Leesburg Pike and later given the name of its owner, Hachaliah Bailey, is now an overpass on Leesburg Pike. Vienna, McLean, and Herndon, longtime pastoral communities, are now teeming with residential and commercial development. (Vienna Station, western terminus of the Metro Transit System, is scheduled to begin operating in 1986.) The Lake Barcroft community developed in the 1950s around a lake which formed after a dam was built in 1913 on Holmes Run by Alexandria City's Water Company has been completely encircled by newer communities. Reston, a newer and larger community, also developed around a lake was founded in the late 1960s. Clifton, begun as a 19th century railroad station in western Fairfax County, was proposed in the 1960s as an all-encompassing city taking in all of Fairfax County and swallowing up local jurisdictions. Fairfax City, which for over two centuries has been the seat of county government, has lost all vestiges of its early agricultural beginnings.

Alexandria's inner city has been converted into graceful open plazas and colonial style modern buildings. Remaining from the past is the 18th century *Carlyle House,* now a museum, believed to have been built over the 17th century fort constructed by the area's earliest colonists for protection against Indians. Today oceangoing vessels only occasionally dock at what was in earlier times one of the area's major ports.

A phenomenon of Northern Virginia has been the development of military and civilian agencies devoted to research and development. Many computer and data processing businesses under government contract are also located along the highways most accessible to the nation's capital. The Tyson's-Dulles corridor as far out as Chantilly could well become the nation's next "Silicon Valley."

In the year 1900 the total population of Arlington, Fairfax, and Alexandria was 39,538 persons. That same year the community of Bailey's Crossroads contained 95 people. In 1985, the population of suburban Northern Virginia which comprises approximately 450 square miles is estimated at close to 1 million persons and still growing. Bailey's Crossroads, encompassing but six square miles, has 31,000 of this number, nearly one-third of whom live in twenty-story condominiums at Skyline Towers.

Not only has the population grown but its composition has been changed. Northern Virginia is caught up in a second great wave of immigrants. The first wave in the preceding centuries came primarily from Europe; this one comes from the Orient, the Caribbean, the Middle East, and the Asian subcontinent. In 1985, the sight of a turbaned man followed by his wife clad in a sari or loose pantaloons, or a Middle Easterner in native dress, scarcely merits a second glance. This then has been the destiny of Northern Virginia—to be a crossroads of history.

APPENDIX A

Simon Pearson's Patent

Fairfax Court House Deed Books A-2, page 270; A-2, 450; L-2, 394; O-2, 189; D-3, 395; and H-3, 192 contain information about the land tract called "Simon Pearson's Patent dated February 17, 1729."

The Patent of Simon Pearson: A Summary

1729-1733

Simon Pearson, whose father's interests in plantation lands had created wealth, lived at Aquia Creek, Virginia. Just as his father Thomas had done, Captain Simon Pearson acquired a great deal of land in the Falls Church-Alexandria area. On February 17, 1729, he obtained another tract by patent from Lord Fairfax, 330 acres of the land now lying between Bailey's Crossroads and Four Mile Run. Captain Simon was a doting father, bequeathing vast land tracts, money, jewels and slaves to his wife and children who were either related to, or were to marry into, many of the families famous in Alexandria-Arlington-Fairfax County history.

1733-1773

Susannah Pearson, Simon's daughter who married John Alexander III, inherited the 330 acres land patent. John and

Susannah built a home on the south bank of Four Mile Run, the exact site of which is not now known since John and Susannah owned several land tracts. When John died, the 330 acre tract passed to the ownership of John Luke.

1773

John Luke, Sr., was related to the family of William Fitzhugh who had owned the nearby Fairfax County plantation *Ravensworth.* John presented his 330 acre acquisition to his son, John Luke, Jr., and his bride, Elizabeth. John and Elizabeth continued the development of the plantation's farmlands and lived in a Mansion House which stood near Long Branch and Leesburg Road. Near the mansion was a body of water called Whortleberry Pond.

1797

John Luke, Jr., leased a house on Leesburg Road to innkeeper Jacob Bontz. Bontz, leasing the house for twenty years, operated it as the Tavern Hotel.

1798

John Luke, Jr., mortgaged the entire property for 1712 pounds, 13 shillings, Maryland money, paid by William Magruder and Thomas Lund Washington of George Town, Joint Merchants and Co-partners in trade under the name and firm of Magruder and Company.

1799

On April 3, John Luke and his neighbor, Captain Terrett, accompanied the former U.S. President, General George Washington, who was surveying his land tract which ran along a portion of the eastern boundaries of the properties belonging to Luke, Adams and Terrett. There had been disagreement between Washington and Terrett over the lines between their land tracts and Washington was hoping to clarify the actual boundary lines by means of this survey.

1811

Elizabeth Luke, widowed by John's death, asked Fairfax County authorities to resurvey her property and set aside her Dower Right which was, according to law, one-third of the land. William Payne, the surveyor appointed to do this, drew a 110-acre plat of Elizabeth Luke's Dower which contained her Mansion House, Bontz' Tavern, and a smaller third house. The survey seems to indicate that the mansion stood at *Maury's* site, that Bontz' Tavern was at Bailey's Crossroads, and that the third house may have been near the site of the present day St. Katherine's Greek Orthodox Church, Glen Carlyn Road. A map of this era designates the site now Bailey's Crossroads as the "fork of the road" made by the road to Cameron (Seminary Road) and the Leesburg-Alexandria Road.

1816

Elizabeth Luke married again to Spencer Ball, Jr., a relative of George Washington and a descendant of the wealthy Carter family which in 1690, when Virginia had 3,000 slaves, owned 1,000 of them. Spencer made an exchange of Elizabeth's Dower, formerly John Luke's property, for property at Harrison, Frederick County, Virginia. The local tract, resurveyed and found to contain not 330 acres but 588¾ acres, was acquired by John Parrell of Frederick County, Virginia.

1817-1837

William Beverley Randolph, son of David Meade Randolph of Presque Isle, Virginia, a relative of the illustrious Virginia family, was the next owner. William, born in 1789, was Lieutenant of Cavalry during the War of 1812. In May 1816, he married Sarah Lingan, daughter of General James Macubbin Lingan. In September 1817, when William and Sarah's first child, James Lingan Randolph, was three months old, they purchased from Parrell for $500.00 the entire land tract which was still being called "The Patent of Simon Pearson dated February 17, 1729." In April 1818, Randolph paid the mortgage which was owed Magruder and others.

Sarah's father, General Lingan, had been a founder of Georgetown when it was incorporated in 1789, and he became the Collector for the George Town Port. He built a rambling frame house on Spring Hill to the west of Georgetown Observatory overlooking Georgetown Port, the canal and Washington City. When the General was killed while trying to quell Federalist rioters in Baltimore in 1812, a 363-ton ship under construction at Georgetown was named the "General Lingan." Lingan's house was later purchased by Mr. Foxhall for whom Foxhall Road was to be named.

Some of the timber used for ship building at Georgetown and Alexandria during the Federalist period may have come from

Bailey's area and may have inspired the building of long frame houses. The central part of the house known as *Maury* resembled the Randolph family's ancestral home in Southern Virginia, so it may have been William and Sarah Randolph who made a wood addition to an older brick colonial dwelling.

Nine other Randolph children were born: Martha Jane, 1818; William Moray (sometimes Maury), 1821; Emma Beverly, 1823; Cornelia Patterson, 1825; Richard, 1827; Mary Meade, 1828, who married W. W. Turner of the Smithsonian Institution; Harriet Isabel, 1830; Elizabeth Gibbon, 1833, who married Washington Custis Calvert of Maryland; and David Meade, 1836.

William Beverley Randolph became the Chief Clerk of the U.S. Treasury Department, which was the Civil Service GS-18 of his day. On August 31, 1837, his infant son David Meade died, and William decided to sell his country property. During the twenty years the Randolphs owned it, the Leesburg Turnpike was improved. The Washington Gravelled Turnpike, now called Columbia Pike, was begun in 1809 and completed for use by traveling animals. The crossing of these pikes created an important landmark.

Another son, James Lingan Randolph, became a civil engineer and built a home for his family near Jessups, Maryland, which he named *Moray*. His father, William Beverley Randolph, died in 1868 and was buried at Georgetown, D.C.

1837-1843

Hachaliah and Mary Bailey of Westchester County, N.Y., purchased on December 19, 1837, the entire Pearson Patent from Randolph, except for small tracts which had been sold to Lawrence Lacy and Wesley Adams. Hachaliah, a wealthy showman, cattleman, and hotel proprietor, with extensive investments in circus menageries and steamboats, paid $6,000.00 for 526 acres. He bestowed his name on Bailey's Crossroads which he had acquired for wintering circus animals.

1843

Mariah Bailey, wife of Lewis Bailey, was deeded the entire tract purchased by her father-in-law, Hachaliah Bailey, on April 18, 1843. Born in 1807, Mariah, a talented equestrienne, was matriarch and businesswoman of Bailey's Crossroads for over fifty years until her death in 1896. Her descendants and descendants of her associates living today remember her with affection and admiration!

APPENDIX B

The Lewis Bailey Family

On April 3, 1883, Mariah Bailey wrote to her former neighbor, Lucinda Bray Barcroft, wife of Dr. Barcroft, who had returned to New Jersey for a while: "... We have raised a family of 10 children, lived here about 40 years and spent for doctors' bills, in sickness, not over $50." (Letter in possession of the Barcroft's great-grand-daughter, Mrs. Jonathan T. Rorer.)

For her children's early education, Mariah hired a tutor from Britain to stay at *Maury* prior to the Civil War. Also each Bailey son was expected to learn a particular skill which would help in running the family businesses.

During the early years at Bailey's, Mariah and Lewis were very interested in maintaining blood lines in their horses. Mariah's equestrienne ability was outstanding and, through her training, her sons became expert riders. Although showmanship, veterinarian education, and other skills were acquired from the wintering activities of traveling wagon shows, the Bailey boys grew up as observers and not as participants of circus life.

The Baileys became well known in Maryland and Virginia as they entered competition at horse shows and fairs. Mariah entered her sons in competition when they were scarcely out of the cradle. There were many awards to various family members in recognition of animal training and riding skills. A silver cup awarded to young Horace is particularly treasured. It is engraved: "Presented to

Horace Upton Bailey, Age 5 years, by the Maryland State Agriculture Society, 1850."

By 1860, Lewis set the high evaluation on the Crossroads property of $20,000.00 for real estate and $2,500.00 for personal property. (U. S. Census, National Archives, 1860.) As each child came of age, Mariah and Lewis presented him or her with a house on a tract of land:

Harvey Bailey, born 1829, farmed near Glebe Road on Columbia Pike. He married Sarah Elizabeth Jenks, daughter of William Jenks, inventor of a breech-loading gun.

Walter T. Bailey, born 1837, became a landscape gardener.

Theodore Bailey, born 1838, became a carpenter. Theodore's son, *Edgar,* who died in 1955, was the last member of the family to live at the Crossroads.

William Bailey, born 1841, operated the Bailey's Dairy Stand at old Rigg's Market, D.C.

Ray Tompkins Bailey, born 1843, became a blacksmith and wheelwright. His second marriage was to Mary Gordon, daughter of Daniel and Amanda Gordon.

Horace Upton Bailey, born 1845, became a veterinarian. He married Eliza Gordon, sister of Mary Gordon.

George F. Bailey, born in 1847, was named for a relative who owned and managed the George F. Bailey Circus and was a manager of the Barnum and Bailey's Circus. Some believe that this younger George F. was also associated for a while with these circuses. In later years he represented a South American fruit company which introduced tropical fruits to the United States. It is known that he traveled extensively before his death from tuberculosis in 1891. The headstone at George F. Bailey's grave near other family members' graves is the tallest monument in the Falls Church Cemetery.

A niece, Dora Bailey Terrett, recalls the last days of George F.: "He was rather dapper, always dressed in the latest fashion, wearing spats and carrying a goldheaded walking cane." She remembers a large oil painting of George in which he was posed beside an array of fruit. The picture hung in George F.'s Crossroads house which he bequeathed to his sister, Elizabeth Francis of Connecticut.

Henry Bailey, born 1849. operated a Crossroads store.

Oscar Bailey raised oranges at Columbia, Georgia, for shipment north. In later years he and his brothers occasionally visited Sarasota where large American circuses wintered.

Daughter *Elizabeth Francis* lived in Connecticut. In the 1880s and 1890s she and her daughters spent summers at *Maury,* much to Mariah's contentment.

MARIAH BAILEY — In Memoriam

Mariah Bailey's image has dimmed, but memory of her persists in some of her land transactions. The first St. Paul's Episcopal Chapel, now an antique store, was built on two acres of ground provided by Mariah to Episcopal Seminary in 1886. Theodore Bailey was hired to construct a chapel with a belfry. Mariah contributed carriage houses formerly used by Crossroads Inn guests to the chapel. These were extended across the back of the chapel building to create the traditional cross shape of nave and chancel. Young seminarians from Episcopal Seminary rode on horseback along Seminary Road to hold services in the new chapel and usually ate dinner at *Maury* boarding house during the chapel's earliest years.

Bailey's Elementary School was built in the 1870s on land at the Crossroads deeded by Mariah to Fairfax County. The original frame building was replaced in 1901 by the present red brick. From 1960 until 1964, it was used as the first home of the University of Virginia's George Mason College.

Horace Bailey's daughters, Marguerite Gordon Bailey and Marie Blackford Cartwright, together with their numerous cousins, remember pleasant childhood days. A favorite destination for a twilight stroll with father Horace was the stone memorial commemorating Lincoln's Review of the Army. This marker was placed there by a historical society but was lost during building in the 1950s. The children found many Indian relics in the Bailey-Munson fields, enough to fill a burlap sack.

An especially exciting pastime in the 1890s, pursued by Theodore's daughter Dora Bailey Terrett and her friends, was hunting for an elephant's grave. Her father had told her about the death of an elephant while its circus had wintered at Bailey's. The elephant had been buried somewhere in the Glen Forest area, its grave marked with rocks. Theodore did not tell the children exactly where the grave was located which prolonged the fun for all in the game known locally as "Old Elephant Bones."

An elephant's capture did take place at Bailey's Crossroads in the early 1900s. The Luna Amusement Park near present-day Shirlington had obtained an elephant act. A storm blew up on the night of the first show, causing a stampede of terrified elephants. Trumpeting wildly during the thunder and lightning, one of the animals crashed his way up the slopes from Four Mile Run to Bailey's where he was lassoed in a cornfield. When all the elephants were rounded up, the owners left hastily, leaving irate farmers to contemplate damage done to crops!

The old circular riding ring was still in use during the early years of the 20th century. The local area provided trails for cyclists and horseback riders from Washington, especially during the Presidential term of Theodore Roosevelt. A carriage ride or brisk trot from the White House to Bailey-Munson's was a favored excusion for Roosevelt in his earnest pursuit of physical fitness.

Two brothers who were related to Dr. Barcroft, Milton and Frank Payne, lived at Bailey-Munson's. Edward Payne, a descendant of William Adams, lived at Church Hill House. Luther Payne operated a Crossroads store. Thomas Terrett ran another store. Other friends and neighbors were named Munson, Row, Lane, Torreyson, Ball, Hunter, Oliver, Head, Mortimer, O'Shaughnessy, Gorham, and Gaines.

In 1913, Alexandria's Water Company built a dam near the mill formerly belonging to Dr. Barcroft. The dam drastically changed the watercourse of the Holmes Run tributaries.

Many people, including Marguerite and Marie, remember the night the old house on Munson Hill burned. The girls watched from their bedroom window in Horace's house beside *Maury* as flames seared the night sky to the west. The accidental burning of *Pendennis* was the end of the first Munson house. Families named Gray and Patterson lived in the house before it burned. How far back in local history this house goes, no one knows. In the early 20th century, the ancient house was referred to as the "old place."

Marguerite's father, Horace Bailey, had many vivid recollections of earlier days at Bailey's for his children. There had been prancing horses in fancy harnesses, painted wagons (some with gold trim), and big lumbering elephants. Mariah's descendants always spoke proudly of her and her ability to ride "circus style." They were also proud of Hachaliah whom P. T. Barnum called Father of the American Circus in his autobiography.

Marguerite Bailey attended a resident school in Georgetown, and after graduation stayed on to live there. As long as Eliza and Horace lived, she visited them on weekends and sat on the verandah to discuss horses in the news and recent horse shows. Now none of her relatives live at the Crossroads.

APPENDIX C

Freedman John Bell

After the Civil War, one of Timothy Munson's sons married and built his home on a fifty-five-acre tract on Columbia Pike near Barcroft's mill. While his family was still young, tragedy struck: fire destroyed the homestead, burning to death a beloved young daughter. Only a large hollow oak tree, pitted to the roots by the fire, was left standing at the site. Stricken with grief, the family moved elsewhere after deeding five acres to their family cook and disposing of the rest to a freedman named John Bell.

John Bell had been born in the Blue Ridge area of the South. One of his parents had been Cherokee and an earlier ancestor white. After the turbulent days of the War and Emancipation, John, educated by a former master, headed for Washington. He became devoted to the faith of the Baptist Church. His ancestral ties to the Blue Ridge of southern Virginia, North Carolina, and East Tennessee brought him back to visit many times. He noted that many blacks did not like to be relegated to seats in the balconies or back rows of churches. This made him determined to help them organize their own Baptist churches.

Traveling on horseback from community to community through the Blue Ridge and Tidewater Counties of Virginia and North Carolina, John pursued his goal with single-minded enthusiasm. Even after organizing churches, he would revisit them frequently.

When not on tour, he was at the Baptist headquarters for freedmen in Washington.

After John married, he looked for a country place near Washington which would be on a road leading to points south and west. The burned-out property of Munson was the answer to his needs. The Bell family of seven daughters and two sons, and many of the grandchildren, grew up in the Bell homestead which John Bell built (at the present site of Barcroft View Apartments).

Many neighbors of the Bells had descended from local slave families. In the late 19th century, new families moved into the area. Two of the earliest families to own property at the Crossroads were the Williamses and the Walkers, the latter having been descendants of Mary Donaldson whose property adjoined that of John Bell.

Upon the death of the aged Munson cook, the Shepperd family acquired her land. The Marshalls and Banks had homes on the bluffs above Holmes Run. The Hunters who lived at Munson Hill (site of J. E. B. Stuart High School and County Park) and the Footes (site of Seven Corners Shopping Center) obtained acreage called Manumition Tracts.

In 1869, a Baptist Church was organized at nearby Mt. Pleasant near Mason's Hill. In the early 1920s, a split in this church resulted in the organization of the Warner Baptist Church which built a small building on a part of the estate of a white real estate broker named Warner who deeded land at Bailey's Crossroads to the congregation.

Interested in education as well as religion, John Bell provided a five-acre tract near Columbia Pike for public school use in the 1880s. One of Fairfax County's first public schools, this small frame building was used for several years by black children until it was closed and the tract reverted to Bell ownership as John's deed specified.

During the early decades of the 20th century, no local school was provided for black students. For a few years, children walked to a one-room school at Mt. Pleasant where youthful Mrs. Lillian Carey was principal. In the 1920s, a school at Bailey's Crossroads with Mrs. Carey as principal held classes in the Warner Church building and then moved into a small frame school building which was built and operated by the county until it was closed in 1940. Thereafter, students went by bus to school in Falls Church until the brick Lillian Carey Elementary School was built in 1959 at Bailey's Crossroads.

Julia Bell, one of John's granddaughters, grew up in the Bell homestead. Her favorite playhouse had been the large hollowed oak beside the burned Munson homesite. She remembers the fun of skating while hanging onto slow-moving farm wagons, once Columbia Pike in front of Grandfather Bell's house had been paved after World War I.

Julia married the Reverend Milton Shepperd, pastor of Warner and Mt. Pleasant Baptist Churches. Mt. Pleasant Church, one of the oldest churches in Fairfax County, celebrated 96 years of existence in 1965. Mr. Shepperd served for 10 years as President of the Fairfax County Chapter of the National Association for the Advancement of Colored People. The Shepperds' brick home on Shepperd's Court is near the site of the homestead land tract of John Bell.

BIBLIOGRAPHY

Backus, Hadassah, *Recollections of a Nativeborn Glen Carlynite,* MS, 1958.

Ballantine, Bill, *Wild Tigers and Tame Fleas,* Rinehart, 1958.

Bannister, *Glossary of Cornish Names,* Williams and Norgate, London, 1871.

Barnard, J. G., Bvt. Major General, U. S. Engineers, *Defences of Washington,* #20, Professional Papers of the Corps of Engineers, U. S. Army, National Archives, 1871.

Barnum, P. T., *My Autobiography,* enlarged edition, Hartford, 1869.

Bethlehem Good Housekeeping Club, Manassas, Va., *Prince William, The Story of Its People and Its Places,* Whittet & Shepperson, reprint 1961.

Billingsley, Frances and Williams, Edgar I., *The Elephant Hotel,* Somers Historical Society, Somers, N. Y., 1962.

Brooks, *The Last Migrations,* Handlet Press, N. Y., 1924.

Catton, Bruce, *The Coming Fury,* Doubleday, & Co., 1961.

Coup, W. C., *Sawdust and Spangles,* Stone & Co., 1901.

Falkner, Leonard, *A Monster Lived At Somers,* New York World Telegram and Sun, Sept. 24, 1963.

Fenwick, Mary Virginia, *Historic Munson Hill,* MS., 1895.

Fairfax County, Office of Research and Statistics, *Fairfax County Profile,* 1982.

Fitzpatrick, John C., *Diaries of George Washington 1748-1749,* Houghton Miflin Co., 1925.

Harrison, Fairfax, *Mrs. Browne's Diary in Virginia and Maryland, 1754-1757,* Virginia Historical Society, Vol. 32.

Harrison, Fairfax, *Old Prince William,* Vols. I and II, 1924, reprint, Chesapeake Publishing Co., Berryville, Va., 1963.

Haydon, F. Stansbury, *Aeronautics in the Union and Confederate Armies,* Vol. I, Johns Hopkins Press, 1941.

Hening's Statutes on Colonial Records, 1820, Vol. 2, Sept. 20, 1674 and Oct. 1677.

Hopkins, G. M., *Atlas of 15 Miles Around Washington,* Phila. 1879.

Hulbert, Archer Butler, *Indian Thoroughfares,* A. H. Clark Co., 1902.

Isenburg, Arthur, *My Town and the Big Top,* MS., 1954.

Jones, Virgil Carrington, *Gray Ghosts and Rebel Raiders,* 1956.

Kimmel Stanley, *Mr. Lincoln's Washington,* Bramhall House, N. Y., 1957.

Leech, Margaret, *Raveille in Washington,* Harper and Brothers, 1941.

Lee, Dorothy Ellis, *A History of Arlington County, Virginia,* Dietz, 1946.

Lindsey, Mary, *Historic Homes and Landmarks of Alexandria,* 1962.

McClure, Stanley W., *The Defenses of Washington, 1861-1865,* National Capital Parks, reprint, 1961.

Mitchell, Beth, *Beginning at a White Oak,* 1977 Fairfax County Administrative Services.

Moore, Ardela, *Bailey's Grand Review,* American Motorist Magazine, April, May, 1930.

Munson, Myron, *The Munson Record,* Vol. II, 1895.

Netherton, N.; Sweig, D.; Artemal, J.; Hickin, P.; Reed, P.; *Fairfax County, A History;* Fairfax County Board of Supervisors, 1978.

Netherton, R.; Waldeck, R.; *The Fairfax County Courthouse,* Fairfax County Office of Comprehensive Planning, 1977.

Odell, Rice, *We Kept Moving Out of the Way,* Washington Daily News, April 5, 1963.

Official Rebellion Records of the Union and Confederate Armies, Va. 51 Part 1, Serial 107, page 38.

Ordinance of Secession, published by Fairfax County Library, 1963.

Peters, Harry, *Currier & Ives,* Doubleday-Doran, 1942.

Proctor, John Clagget, *Proctor's Washington,* 1949.

Records of Long Standing, 1742-1770, Records Room, Fairfax
    Court House.
Robinson, Gil, *Wagon Show Days,* Brockwell Co., 1925.
Rose, C. B., Jr., *Indians of Arlington,* pub. by Office of County
    Manager, Arlington, Va., 1957.
Steadman, Melvin, Jr., *The Virginian, Falls Church Echo News-
    paper, Nov. 11, 1949.*
Steadman, Melvin, Jr., Falls Church by Fence and Fireside, Falls
    Church Public Library, 1964.
Stephenson, Richard W., *Civil War Maps, An Annotated List,* 1961,
    Library of Congress.
Stepp and Hill, ed., *Mirror of War: The Washington Star Reports the
    Civil War,* 1961.
Stetson, Charles, *Four Mile Run Land Grants,* Mimeoform Press,
    1935.
Stetson, Charles, *Washington and His Neighbors,* Garret &
    Massey, 1956.
Sturtevant, C. G., *White Tops,* Vol. 17, Nos. 11, 12, 1944.
Templeman, Eleanor Lee, *Arlington Heritage,* 1959.
Virginia: A Guide to the Old Dominion, W. P. A., Oxford Press, N. Y.,
    1940.
Wallace, Irving, *The Fabulous Showman—P. T. Barnum,* Knopf,
    1959.
Wilson, Mitchell, *American Science and Invention,* Simon &
    Schuster, 1954.
Wilson, Rufus Rockwell, *Washington, The Capital City,* Vol. I,
    Lippincott, 1901.
Wilstach, Paul, *Potomac Landings,* Tudor Publishing Co., N. Y.,
    1937.

FOOTNOTES

CHAPTER 2

[1] *Hening's Statutes of Colonial Records, 20 September 1674.*

[2] *Ibid., October 1677.*

[3] *Diaries of George Washington, 1748-1799, Vol. IV 1789-1799,* John C. Fitzpatrick, ed., Houghton Mifflin Co. *for the Mt. Vernon Ladies Association of the Union, 1925*

[4] In 1917, the Fairfax County Chapter of the Daughters of the American Revolution erected an iron fence around milestone #6 SW, which by that date was badly battered and chipped. Mrs. T. P. O'Shaughnessey, who at that time owned land at the site, deeded the fenced portion to the Virginia DAR. In 1960, the stone was removed to make way for a new apartment building and Arlington County Officials rescued the stone and stored it in the basement of Arlington County Court House. In 1965, the 174-year-old marker was reset through the cooperation of the Arlington County Cultural and Heritage Commission near the original site at South Jefferson Street at Columbia Pike. A rededication in July, 1965 marked this event.

[5] *Falls Church by Fence and Fireside,* Melvin Lee Steadman, paragraph 221-239

[6] Church Hill property, refurbished after having been damaged during the Civil War, was owned by descendants of the Adams-Lipscomb-Payne family until it was sold in 1924. At this time it was enlarged and remodeled. Until the 1940s, the King's Seal, which belonged to a former surveyor of lands patented by Lord Fairfax, hung over the front door.

The seal is now missing. The house, occupied continuously for 210 years until 1960, stood behind J. E. B. Stuart High School until destroyed for apartment buildings in 1964. The framework of a mantel had been removed and placed in Dulin Methodist Church, Falls Church. It is believed the earliest cemetery of the family lies deeply buried under the high school's athletic field, undisturbed because the field was raised to a height above the original elevation.

CHAPTER 3

[1] Fairfax County Deed Book, D-3, p. 395.

[2] Fairfax County Deed Book, H-3, page 192.

[3] *The Munson Record,* Vol. II Myron Munson, 1896, Library of Congress.

[4] Bruce Catton, *The Coming Fury;* 1961; Doubleday and Co.

CHAPTER 4

[1] Carl Sandburg, *Life of Lincoln.*

[2] Bruce Catton, *The Coming Fury;* 1961.

[3] *The Daily Picayune,* 24 July 1861.

[4] Percy Smith, "Ball's Crossroads;" Arlington Historical Magazine, Oct. 1960, p. 47.

[5] Mary Virginia Fenwick Lane, Historic Munson Hill, unpublished manuscript[1]

[6] Ibid.

[7] Official Rebellion Record of the Union and Confederate Armies, Vir. 51, Part 1, Serial #107, p. 38.

[8] Professional Papers of the Corps of Engineers, U. S. Army, 1871, #20, p. 4, National Archives.

[9] Washington Star, September 30, 1861.

[10] Proctor's Washington, John Clagett Procter, 1949.

CHAPTER 5

[1] The Munson Record, 1896, Miles Munson.

[2] *The Daily Picayune,* July 1861.

[3] National Archives, Claims file, #92-181, Box 299.

[4] 3rd Auditor, #1764, Maria Bailey, July 9, 1878, War Record Group 217, National Archives.

[5] Letters from William Robinson to his wife Emily, 1865, in the possession of Mr. and Mrs. W. P. McGowan.

CHAPTER 6

[1] The Munson Record, 1896, Miles Munson.
[2] Wallace, Irving, *The Fabulous Showman—P. T. Barnum,* Knopf, 1959.
[3] American Motorist Magazine, May 1930.